D0065394

Presented To

_____

On

_____

By

_____

LIFE ON PURPOSE™ DEVOTIONAL FOR MEN

*Practical Faith and Profound Insight
for Every Day*

By
J.M. Farro

Harrison House
Tulsa, OK

09 08 07 06 05   10 9 8 7 6 5

Life on Purpose™ Devotional for Men:
Practical Faith and Profound Insight for Every Day
ISBN 1-57794-648-0
Copyright © 2004 by J.M. Farro
P.O. Box 434
Nazareth, PA 18064

Published by Harrison House, Inc.
P.O. Box 35035
Tulsa, OK 74153

Contents

Our God-Given Purpose

The Lord will fulfill his purpose for me.

PSALM 138:8

I like to declare this Bible verse every day. Because I've committed my life to God, this Scripture reassures me that His purpose for my life will prevail. Many people spend years setting goals and making plans, only to discover that what they thought they wanted wasn't what they wanted at all. Nowadays, a lot of people think that getting more and more education is the answer to their search for fulfillment. Often they realize too late that all the education in the world can't guarantee they'll be truly satisfied in the end. It never occurred to them to ask God what *His* plans for them were. They weren't aware of the fact that He created them with a specific purpose in mind, and that if they aligned their plans with His, they would experience a peace and contentment that can be attained no other way.

If you will wholeheartedly commit your life to the Lord and cooperate with His plans for you, He will move mountains to ensure that His purpose for your life is fulfilled. You may be an artist, and people have told you there is already too much competition in the art world. The odds are stacked against you, so don't waste your time, they may say. Perhaps you're a musician, and everyone says you'd better pick another profession because there are already too many people in the music business. Maybe God has given you a vision to go into some form of ministry, but you're being told that you'll starve. Or you're feeling overwhelmed

LIVE ON PURPOSE TODAY

What is in your heart that you've always wanted to do? What fills you with excitement and energy? Sometimes the desires in our hearts are actually placed there by God. Write those things down and commit them to prayer.

because it seems that God is leading you into the medical profession, but all you can think about are the many years and costs of education ahead of you. Listen carefully. If it's your sincere desire to fulfill your God-given purpose in life, and you believe that God is calling you into the ministry, the music business, or anywhere else—rest assured that He will make a way where there seems to be none. You will find satisfaction and joy in your labor. And no power on earth or in hell itself will be able to keep God's blessings from you!

PRAYER

Lord, I offer you all that I am and all that I have, and I ask that You fulfill Your purpose for me. Show me what my God-given gifts are, and help me to use them for Your glory. Bless all the work of my hands, and give me favor in the sight of God and man. Give me a right heart so that my motives will always be pleasing to You. Thank You for Your promise which says that I will eat the fruit of my labor, and blessings and prosperity shall be mine!

Rejoicing in Our Labor

{ *To enjoy your work and accept your lot in life—*
that is indeed a gift from God. }

ECCLESIASTES 5:19 NLT

Over the years I had read this verse many times, but about a month ago, the Lord began shedding some new light on it for me. For as long as I can remember, I had this notion that I shouldn't expect to enjoy my work, and that I should approach much of my labor with a "grin and bear it" kind of attitude. And what was to convince me otherwise? It seemed that I was always surrounded by people who shared and demonstrated that exact mindset. But recently the Lord began showing me the above verse and others like them, and dealing with me about my wrong thinking in this area. He led me to begin praying and standing on these truths for myself and my loved ones, and He has already begun to reward my faith with exciting new work-related blessings for all of us.

The Bible makes it abundantly clear that God wants us to enjoy our work. Solomon puts it plainly when he says, "To enjoy your work...that is indeed a gift from God" (Eccl. 5:19 NLT). This is a common theme throughout the Book of Ecclesiastes. Solomon also writes, "That everyone may eat and drink, and find satisfaction in all his toil—this is the gift of God" (Eccl. 3:13). So now that we know that God wants us to find joy and satisfaction in our work—and that these are gifts from Him—what can we do? We can ask Him for them, trusting that He is true to His Word when

He says that whenever we pray in line with His will, He will answer us. (1 John 5:14,15.) Jesus said, "If you, then, though you are evil, know how to give good gifts to your children, how much more will your Father in heaven give good gifts to those who ask him!" (Matt. 7:11). And James wrote, "You do not have, because you do not ask God" (James 4:2). The key word in these verses is *ask*. Don't assume that you have to settle for doing distasteful and unfulfilling work all your life. Yes, there may be times when we might have to endure some periods of doing work we dislike, but our prayer and our goal should be to spend most of our lives doing the kind of work that gives us joy. One of my regular prayers for myself and my family is, "Lord, please enable us to earn a good living doing what we love to do most." I also pray that God will help us to do our part in the fulfillment of this prayer. One way we can cooperate with the Lord to this end is to seek His guidance daily, depending on Him to keep us in His perfect will. When we're doing what God has called us to do, we will experience a peace, joy, and satisfaction that will be missing when we're out of His will.

LIVE ON PURPOSE TODAY

Enjoying your work is, indeed, a gift from God. So, graciously accept the Lord's gift and begin thanking Him for the reality of it to come to pass in your life!

I encourage you to begin asking God to make a way for you to enjoy your work. If you're in a position where you really dislike your job or the work you're doing, the Lord can open up a new door of opportunity for you as a result of your prayers. If it's not His will and timing for you to make a move right now, He can make your present job more pleasant and fulfilling somehow. He may do that by causing you to find favor or recognition in the sight of your employer or coworkers. Or He may improve your working conditions in various little ways until He can move you into a more desirable position. But rest assured that as you pray in faith, God will do *something* to enable you to enjoy your labor more. If you're a child of God, you don't have to resign yourself to a "grin and bear it" attitude toward your work. God has made a way for you to find joy and satisfaction in your toil. May you begin today to press on toward the goal of "rejoicing in your labor"! (Eccl. 5:19 NKJV).

PRAYER

Lord, I believe that it's Your will for me to enjoy my work. Please teach me how to do that. Keep me in Your perfect will so that I'll always be in the right place at the right time, even where my work is concerned. Thank You for enabling me to earn a good living doing what I love to do!

Our Rightful Source

This is what the Lord says: "Cursed is the one
who trusts in man, who depends on flesh for his
strength and whose heart turns away from the Lord....
But blessed is the man who trusts in the Lord, whose
confidence is in him. He will be like a tree planted
by the water that sends out its roots by the stream...."

JEREMIAH 17:5,7,8

I like the way God doesn't mince words. He makes it abundantly clear that He wants us to put our trust in Him and not man. He goes so far as to say that those who put their trust in people will be cursed. Isaiah 2:22 says, "Stop trusting in man, who has but a breath in his nostrils. Of what account is he?" I especially like the way David puts it in Psalm 60:11: "Give us aid against the enemy, for the help of man is worthless." And for those of us who are tempted to put our trust in leaders, Psalm 146:3 says, "Do not put your trust in princes, in mortal men who cannot save." But the verses above reassure us that those who put their trust in God will not have to fear or worry even in a year of drought, because they will always be fresh and fruitful!

A job can be a good thing, but God doesn't want us making it our source. If we do, when we lose it, we will have no means of support. On the other hand, if we make God our provider, even if we are jobless for a time, our needs will still be met. Doctors can definitely be a blessing. But if we rely only on their limited wisdom and leave God out of the picture, it could cost us our health—maybe even our lives. Spouses and parents can be wonderful gifts, but depending on them for all our needs can be disastrous if they're ever taken from us. The good news is that God is willing and able to be all that we need in this life. If you are looking for stability and security in this ever-changing world, make our unchangeable God the source of all your needs. Then you can exclaim with the psalmist, "O Lord Almighty, blessed is the man who trusts in you"! (Ps. 84:12).

LIVE ON PURPOSE TODAY

Take time today to think about those you rely on. Would you be devastated if they were removed from your life? Reflect on Psalm 146:3. Begin to ask God to build your faith and ability to trust and rely on Him for your every need.

PRAYER

Lord, forgive me for the times I put my trust in man, rather than in You. Help me to look to You for all my needs, including all my physical, emotional, and spiritual needs. Help me to realize that when I make You my source, my resources are boundless. Thank You that no matter what happens, I will always be blessed and fruitful!

Can You Pray?

Keep alert and pray. Otherwise temptation will overpower you.
For though the spirit is willing enough, the body is weak!

MATTHEW 26:41 NLT

O nce when I was confessing my sins to the Lord and telling Him how powerless I felt to overcome my sinful behavior, I heard Him ask, "Can you pray?" I immediately felt convicted and knew in my heart what He was trying to tell me. The truth of the matter was that I was not completely helpless in my sinful state. God had provided me with a powerful weapon that I could make use of no matter how inadequate I felt: It was a simple thing called prayer. Jesus told His disciples, "Watch and pray so that you will not fall into temptation. The spirit is willing, but the body is weak" (Matt. 26:41). In fact, in numerous places throughout the Gospels, Jesus instructs us to use prayer as a means of overcoming temptation. He even specifically teaches us to pray, "Lead us not into temptation, but deliver us from the evil one" (Matt. 6:13).

I know what it's like to struggle with temptation and sin, sometimes for years. Often we feel like we're out of control, and we can see no way out of our situation. But I also know what it's like to experience God's supernatural power to heal and deliver. One important part of our ultimate deliverance is confession and repentance. Each time we confess our sin to the Lord, we are agreeing with Him that we have violated His righteous laws, and we are admitting that we need His help to turn away from our sinful behavior. As we repent for our wrongdoing, we are choosing God and His will for us, and as a result, we position ourselves to receive supernatural power to enable us to turn away from our sin. This is exactly why condemnation is such a favorite tool of Satan's. He knows that if he can heap condemnation upon us when we do wrong, he has a good chance of keeping us from going to God for forgiveness and restoration. The psalmist wrote, "If I had not confessed the sin in my heart, my Lord would not have listened. But God did listen! He paid attention to my prayer" (Ps. 66:18,19 NLT). While it's true that our sin can hinder our fellowship with the Lord, it's also true that a sincere sorrow for our sins can restore it.

The Bible is filled with effective prayers we can pray for our deliverance. One of my personal favorites is Psalm 143:10: "Teach me to do Your will, for You are my God; may Your good Spirit lead me on level ground." Another one is Psalm 51:10,12 TLB: "Create in me a new, clean heart, O God, filled with clean thoughts and right desires. Restore to me again the joy of Your salvation, and make me willing to obey You." Praying Scripture-based pleas like these can fill us with a fresh sense of hope. Making positive confessions of faith can also be very helpful. The apostle Paul declared, "I can do all things

LIVE ON PURPOSE TODAY

If you're tired of struggling with the same area of temptation in your life, decide today to change by inviting God into your mind and asking Him to renew your thought patterns. When the trial comes, ask God to take over the situation and provide you a way out. He never intended for us to battle these things alone.

through Christ who strengthens me" (Phil. 4:13 NKJV). When I'm feeling defeated and I confess this Scripture, it reaches down into my soul and lifts me up.

Most of all, we must remember that we are never alone in our struggles against sin. Hebrews 2:18 AMP says of Jesus: "Because He Himself [in His humanity] has suffered in being tempted (tested and tried), He is able [immediately] to run to the cry of (assist, relieve) those who are being tempted and tested and tried [and who therefore are being exposed to suffering]." If we will turn to the Lord in our struggles, if we will depend on His strength rather than our own, and if we will believe that He is willing and able to help and change us, our ultimate victory is assured. Never give up. The devil is a powerful enemy, but your prayers for deliverance have great power, too. Keep praying and believing, and the day will surely come when you will experience for yourself the blessed freedom that only Christ can give!

PRAYER

*Lord, I know that, though You don't ever expect me to be perfect,
You do expect me to always be "pressing toward the mark"
(Phil. 3:14 KJV). When I'm feeling overwhelmed because
of my sinfulness, remind me that because I have put my trust
in Christ, my prayers have "great power and wonderful results"
(James 5:16 NLT). Thank You that You've begun a good work in me,
and You will continue it until Jesus comes back! (Phil. 1:6.)*

Four Steps to Success

Several years ago I heard a godly man offer some advice about how we can enjoy more of the peace and joy that the Lord wants us to have, even in the midst of trouble and uncertainty. He said that if we will make the following statements our personal declarations, and if we will practice the principles behind them, we will gain the victory in every trial we encounter. If we look at each statement in the light of Scripture, we can see that they are all based on sound biblical principles.

1. **"I'm not going to worry about that."** If you've spent any time reading or listening to Scripture, you've undoubtedly become acquainted with the apostle Paul's famous words in Philippians 4: "Don't worry about anything; instead, pray about everything. Tell God what you need, and thank Him for all He has done. If you do this, you will experience God's peace, which is far more wonderful than the human mind can understand. His peace will guard your hearts and minds as you live in Christ Jesus" (Phil. 4:6,7 NLT). Anxiety and worry are rooted in fear, and fear will hinder our faith and trust in God. It will also cause us to lose our sense of direction and make it harder to hear God's "still, small voice." If you're worrying about something, perhaps you need to pray about it more. Keeping it before God in prayer will help you focus more on Him and His abilities, and less on yourself and your inabilities.

2. **"I'm not going to try to figure that out."** One of the hardest things I've had to learn as a true believer in Christ is that I must no longer try to solve my problems my own way. Instead, I must turn to my divine Problem Solver and depend on Him to show me the way. He tells us, "My thoughts are not your thoughts, neither are your ways My ways. As the heavens are higher than the earth, so are My ways higher than your ways and My thoughts than your thoughts" (Isa. 55:8,9). Our thinking is severely limited, while God's is not. Even when we can't find a single solution to our problem, God has more than a million ways to solve it. But He may not reveal the answer until we stop wrestling with the matter and leave it in His hands.

3. **"I'm not going to try to make something happen."** When we're in a trial and it seems like God isn't moving fast enough to suit us, it can be tempting to try to "kick down doors." But we'd be wise to remember that getting ahead of God and trying to make our own way can not only delay our blessings, but keep us from receiving God's best. The fact is that we are more likely to make mistakes when we fail to wait on God, than when we fail to move on His cue. I like to say, "If in doubt, wait." Isaiah had the right idea when he wrote, "The Lord is a faithful God. Blessed are those who wait for Him to help them" (Isa. 30:18 NLT).

LIVE ON PURPOSE TODAY

Begin to declare these statements over your life. When you do this, you are guaranteed success!

4. **"I'm going to trust God!"** Heeding this single foundational biblical principle will help us to avoid all of the obstacles that the previous three statements are designed to overcome. If we're trusting God, we're much less likely to worry, to try to figure things out for ourselves, or to try to make something happen on our own. Scripture says, "Trust in the Lord with all your heart; do not depend on your own understanding. Seek His will in all you do, and He will direct your paths" (Prov. 3:5,6 NLT). If we will turn to God and seek His perfect will for us in every situation—laying aside our own preconceived notions and solutions—we can depend on Him to lead us in the paths of His very best blessings. Best of all, we can have peace and joy while we wait for the Lord's answer, resting in the knowledge that our concerns are in the hands of a mighty and loving God!

PRAYER

Lord, in times of turmoil and uncertainty, help me to put my wholehearted trust in You and Your goodness. Guard me from worry and anxiety, and from trying to figure things out on my own. Teach me how to wait on You and Your perfect timing in everything. Thank You that as I trust and seek You every step of the way, my success is guaranteed!

The Price of Peace Is Prayer

*Do not be anxious about anything, but in everything, by prayer
and petition, with thanksgiving, present your requests to God.
And the peace of God, which transcends all understanding,
will guard your hearts and your minds in Christ Jesus.*

PHILIPPIANS 4:6,7

These verses were the ones that convinced me that God really does want us to pray about everything. Here, Paul tells us that there is nothing in life that we should worry about. Then he says that, instead, we should pray about everything. When I first read these verses, I thought for sure there must be exceptions to the rule. Surely God has better things to do than to listen to my every little complaint or concern. Wrong. Look at it this way—whatever we don't pray about, we're going to worry about, right? And the point God is trying to make here is that He doesn't want us worrying about anything. That means that there's nothing that's too trivial to bring to God's attention in prayer.

Years ago I was told by well-meaning people that I was not to bother God with the little details of life. I have seen many precious people struggle with burdens that God is willing to lighten for them, all because they were under the impression that He's too busy or disinterested in their minor affairs. Now, when I tell you that I pray about everything, you can believe I mean everything. I don't wait until my little problems become big problems. I present them to God right away, and even when He doesn't answer my prayers the way I expect Him to, He always does something to ease the strain. Don't buy into that misconception that says God is not interested in every little detail of your life. Start today to pray about anything and everything that concerns you, and then enjoy the peace and satisfaction that settle over you when you do!

LIVE ON PURPOSE TODAY

What burdens are you carrying around today? Sometimes worries can consume our thoughts. During your drive to work today, pray and turn your cares over to God.

PRAYER

Lord, I'm sorry for all the times I carried burdens I didn't have to, all because I neglected to bring them to You in prayer. Open my eyes and my heart, and help me to see how much You love me and how much You care about every little concern of mine. Whenever I am tempted to shoulder my burdens alone, please remind me to turn to You in prayer, and then surround me with Your perfect, healing peace.

The High Cost of Unforgiveness

> *For if you forgive men when they sin against you, your heavenly Father will also forgive you. But if you do not forgive men their sins, your Father will not forgive your sins.*
>
> MATTHEW 6:14,15

These verses illustrate what is perhaps the best reason for our being forgiving people. Jesus makes it clear that if we don't forgive others, we aren't forgiven by God. How we treat others is a major factor in determining the quality of our relationship with God. Even our prayer life is affected when our attitudes toward others are not right. In Mark chapter 11, when Jesus is teaching about mountain-moving faith, He concludes by saying that if we hold anything against anyone, we must forgive them. If we want our prayers to have power, we cannot hold grudges or harbor bitterness. In Matthew 5:23-24, Jesus tells us that before we offer a gift to God, if we have a grievance against anyone, we need to be reconciled with them. Then God will accept our gift.

If you are holding a grudge against anyone right now, or if you are in strife with anyone, consider this. You could be opening a door for the enemy to come in and destroy your life, marriage, family, or friendships. In 2 Corinthians 2:10-11, Paul talks about forgiving the sinner after the church disciplines him. He says, "And what I have forgiven...I have forgiven in the sight of Christ for your sake, in order that Satan might not outwit us. For we are not

unaware of his schemes."
Paul reveals that by withholding forgiveness we
can give the devil an
advantage over us. I
decided long ago that harboring resentment just
isn't worth it. My relationship with God and my
prayers are too valuable to
me. Maybe you feel you

LIVE ON PURPOSE TODAY

If a relationship has been
broken, take the extra step to
make amends. Look for ways
to rebuild the relationships
that count. Don't allow
the enemy to rob you of
any more valuable time.

have a right to withhold forgiveness from someone. But if you
belong to the Lord, you gave up your rights when you became a
member of His family. Colossians 3:13 says, "Bear with each other
and forgive whatever grievances you may have against one another.
Forgive as the Lord forgave you." How can we refuse to forgive
others when God has so graciously forgiven us? Today, the Savior is
reaching out to you and asking, "Won't you do it for Me?"

PRAYER

Lord, forgive me for all the times I've harbored resentment
toward others. Give me a heart like Yours so that I may be
quick to forgive. When I'm tempted to hold anything against
anyone, remind me how graciously You have forgiven me.
Give me the grace and the wisdom to avoid conversations and
situations that might lead to strife. Thank You that as I practice
forgiveness, I will be blessed with a closer relationship with You!

Prepare for Promotion

Do not despise this small beginning, for the eyes
of the Lord rejoice to see the work begin....

ZECHARIAH 4:10 TLB

A small remnant of Jewish exiles had returned to their homeland after decades of Babylonian captivity. God instructs them to rebuild their temple and their nation. But they become discouraged because of hostilities from their enemies and the realization that the rebuilt temple will not be as great as the previous one, built by King Solomon. The Lord speaks the above words to His weary servants to give them hope and encouragement so that they will continue their God-given task. He tells them that even though it seems like a small beginning, He rejoices in seeing them set to work.

Sometimes God assigns us small tasks which can seem insignificant to us. But in God's sight, there are no unimportant tasks in His kingdom. Sometimes the Lord expects us to prove our faithfulness in little matters before He gives us larger assignments. In Matthew 25:24, Jesus says, "You have been faithful with a few things; I will put you in charge of many things." The Lord is teaching us here that if we will be faithful in the duties He assigns us, promotion will be our reward. At times we can become tempted to promote ourselves, but God's Word makes it clear that job belongs to the Lord. "For promotion and power come from nowhere on earth, but only from God. He promotes one and deposes another" (Ps. 75:6,7 TLB). Perhaps God has given you work to do and you feel as though it has little value or that it's having little impact. Maybe you're receiving very little thanks or recognition. Or you're being met with more resistance than coopera-tion. Perhaps a previous task the Lord had given you was more appealing than the one you're

LIVE ON PURPOSE TODAY

Is there a task—large or small—that you know in your heart the Lord has asked of you? Set about its completion without delay, and set yourself up for promotion from Him!

involved with now. But God doesn't take pleasure in our work for Him only if it's big and important. He rejoices when we do the job He's given us, no matter what the size or significance. If you'll faithfully do the work the Lord's called you to do right now, He will promote you when it will benefit you most. Take heart, for today God's promise to you is—"Humble yourselves, therefore, under God's mighty hand, that he may lift you up in due time"! (1 Peter 5:6).

PRAYER

Lord, forgive me when I feel dissatisfied with the work You've given me to do. Cause me to realize that there are no insignificant tasks in Your kingdom. When I'm tempted to try to promote myself instead of waiting on You, remind me that my efforts will be fruitless in the end. Help me to recognize the jobs You've committed to me and to carry them out faithfully. Thank You that at the proper time You will reward me with promotion!

The Recipe for Success

Commit everything you do to the Lord.
Trust him, and he will help you.

PSALM 37:5 NLT

The Bible contains many promises related to the tasks we perform. The verse above is one of my favorites to pray and stand on whenever I have a job to do. Another one is Proverbs 16:3, "Commit your work to the Lord, and then your plans will succeed." God is eager to bless the work of our hands, and He wants us to succeed in all we do. Notice, though, that He wants us to first entrust our tasks to Him. God wants to be invited into every area of our daily lives, but He is a gentleman. He will not force His help on us. That's not His style. There's a certain amount of humility involved in our asking God for help, and often it's our pride that keeps us from asking. Other times it's the belief that it's not a big enough job to seek God's help with, or it's one that we've performed countless times before. I'm familiar with that way of thinking because I used to think that way myself. Now, no matter how small or insignificant my tasks seem, I ask God for His help, and I believe it pleases Him greatly. How do I know? Because overall, my work goes more smoothly, the results are better, and I experience more joy and satisfaction.

Next time you are doing the yard work or working on your car, invite God to help you. Commit all your child care and parenting duties to Him. Don't try to raise kids these days without the divine assistance that God offers you. Don't try to drive without

Him. Take the Lord along with you when you travel. And why would any child of God want to try to get through school without their heavenly Father's grace, power, and wisdom? If you're employed, bring God to your job each day, and ask Him to help you be the best employee your company's ever had.

LIVE ON PURPOSE TODAY

Purpose to seek God's help in every activity of the day. What one thing immediately comes to mind that you can commit to the Lord right now? As soon as you commit to Him, you've already begun following God's recipe for success!

When you "commit everything you do to the Lord," you will have at your disposal the help of the Father, Son, and Holy Spirit, as well as a legion of angels, if necessary. Today, begin seeking God's help in all your endeavors, and you can bet "the Lord your God will make you successful in everything you do"! (Deut. 30:9 NLT).

PRAYER

Lord, I'm sorry that I've often left You out of my everyday activities. Help me to humble myself and ask You for help with everything I do. When I'm tempted to try to do things on my own, remind me of Your generous offer to help. Deliver me from an independent attitude, and help me to rely on You the way You desire. Thank You for the greater ease, joy, and success I'll find in all my tasks from now on!

When All We Can See Are Giants!

The land we passed through and explored is exceedingly good.
If the Lord is pleased with us, he will lead us into that land,
a land flowing with milk and honey, and will give it to us. Only
do not rebel against the Lord. And do not be afraid of the people
of the land, because we will swallow them up. Their protection
is gone, but the Lord is with us. Do not be afraid of them.

NUMBERS 14:7-9

These are the words of Joshua and Caleb after returning from their exploration of the Promised Land, along with ten other "spies" sent out by Moses, their leader. God had promised the land of Canaan to the Israelites after He delivered them out of the hands of Pharaoh in Egypt. The Lord had told His people that the land He was giving them was lush and fertile—"a land flowing with milk and honey." When the twelve spies scouted out the land in advance, they discovered that "all the people there were of great size" (Num. 13:32), and as a result, ten of the spies brought back a "bad report." Only Joshua and Caleb declared that they were able to conquer the giants, because God was on their side. And because of their faith in God and His promises in the face of certain defeat, they were the only two spies that made it to the Promised Land.

You may have some giants looming in your life right now. They may be financial troubles or health problems, or problems with a parent, child, teacher, or boss. Maybe you've been struggling with your weight for years, and you don't see any way out. Whatever it is, remember Joshua and Caleb. When the other ten spies saw only giants, Joshua and Caleb saw God. There's a song that says, "Turn your eyes upon Jesus." If you'll do that today, God will see to it that you make it to the Promised Land!

LIVE ON PURPOSE TODAY

Identify your giants and find Scriptures in God's Word that promise you victory. Write out one or two Scriptures and carry them with you. Each time the giant situation enters your mind, refer to the Scriptures. Keep standing and you will see your victory in no time!

PRAYER

Lord, You know what I'm up against today. Sometimes my problems seem so big that all I can see is them and not You. Help me to take my eyes off the giants in my life and fix them on You. Cause me to realize how big a God You really are and how willing You are to face all my problems with me, if I'll let You. Thank You that with You beside me, the victory is mine!

Overcoming Anxiety

Don't worry about anything; instead, pray about everything; tell God your needs and don't forget to thank him for his answers. If you do this you will experience God's peace, which is far more wonderful than the human mind can understand. His peace will keep your thoughts and your hearts quiet and at rest as you trust in Christ Jesus.

PHILIPPIANS 4:6,7 TLB

The thesaurus lists "worry, uneasiness, nervousness, tension or stress" as a few synonyms for the word *anxiety*.[1] Fear is at the root of anxiety, and because of that, it's something we need to resist by the power of the Holy Spirit that dwells in us. Anxiety will steal our peace and joy, and that's evidence enough that it's a tool of the enemy. Proverbs 14:30 says, "A heart at peace gives life to the body." The Living Bible puts it this way: "A relaxed attitude lengthens a man's life." Since anxiety robs us of our peace, it can make us susceptible to sickness and disease and take years off our lives. Spend enough time being anxious, and sooner or later you'll be plagued with headaches, stomachaches, backaches, or other ills. The apostle Peter writes, "Cast all your anxiety on [the Lord] because he cares for you" (1 Peter 5:7). God never intended for us to shoulder our own burdens, and trying to do so can have disastrous consequences. Anxiety can also sap our strength and lower our energy levels. As a result, we'll be less productive and fruitful as employees, students, parents, ministers, or anything else we apply ourselves to. Anxiety can even harm our relationships. Those around us can suffer when our anxious thoughts make us short-tempered, depressed, or overly sensitive. If we really care about our friends, family, and others we come in contact with, we'll do our best to walk in peace each day.

The verses we read in Philippians 4 tell us how God wants us to deal with our anxieties and worries. God wants us to acknowledge our need for Him by promptly bringing all our concerns to Him in prayer. Our focus then shifts from our unsettling circumstances to our all-powerful God, who loves us and wants the best for us. As we make a conscious decision to put our trust in the Lord, God's own indescribable peace settles over us and quiets our fears. Isaiah puts it this way: "You will keep in perfect peace all who trust in you, whose thoughts are fixed on you!" (Isa. 26:3). Besides prayer, devoting ourselves to God's Word can counteract anxiety. Psalm 119:165 says, "Those who love your law have great peace and do not stumble." As we meditate on God's faith-building promises, peace and joy spring up inside of us and crowd out anxiety and fear. Psalm 85:8 says, "[The Lord] speaks peace to his people, his saints, if they will only stop their sinning." Sometimes a specific sin is at the root of our anxiety and can

LIVE ON PURPOSE TODAY

Find ten minutes each day to bask in God's peace. Force your mind to rest and refocus on God's promises. Taking just ten minutes each day could improve and extend your life.

keep us from enjoying the peace that God wants us to have. When this is the case, we haven't failed until we've given up trying to be all that God wants us to be. Just before the Savior went to the cross, He gave His disciples a priceless gift. In John 14:27, Jesus says, "I am leaving you with a gift—peace of mind and heart! And the peace I give isn't fragile like the peace the world gives. So don't be troubled or afraid." Our Savior has left us with an unshakable peace which will sustain us in the most difficult times. The apostle Paul confirms this when he says, "May the Lord of peace himself continually grant you peace in every circumstance" (2 Thess. 3:16). Let these words from the Savior encourage your heart today: "Give your entire attention to what God is doing right now, and don't get worked up about what may or may not happen tomorrow. God will help you deal with whatever hard things come up when the time comes" (Matt. 6:34 MESSAGE).

PRAYER

Lord, help me to bring all my cares and anxieties to You in prayer each day so that I won't try to carry them myself. Teach me to trust You and keep my thoughts on You so that I can walk in peace continually. Let it be true of me that "when anxiety was great within me, Your consolation brought joy to my soul"! (Ps. 94:19).

God's Antidote for Disappointment

I am the Lord; those who hope in Me will not be disappointed.

ISAIAH 49:23

I once saw a professional baseball player talking about his faith on television. He spoke about how placing our confidence in people was a mistake, and how we should only put our hope in God. In fact, he made a startling statement like, "People will let us down 100 percent of the time, but God will never let us down." If I had heard him talking like this before I became a committed Christian years ago, I might have thought he was being terribly cynical, but now I know better. The Bible says, "It is better to trust the Lord than to put confidence in people" (Ps. 118:8 NLT). The truth is, whenever we put our confidence in people or become dependent upon them for our needs, we will be disappointed. Only God can make the statement, "Those who hope in Me will not be disappointed," and have it hold true. Jesus did not have a cynical or suspicious nature, and yet He did not put His confidence in people. John 2:24 says, "But Jesus would not entrust himself to them, for he knew all men. He did not need man's testimony about man, for he knew what was in a man." Jesus loved people enough to die for them, but His faith and hope were in God, not man. We need to follow His example.

Years ago I heard a godly man say that whenever we compromise God's Word to gain or keep something or someone, we will lose what we're trying to hold on to. I've learned the hard way that there's a lot of truth to that statement. If you're involved in a relationship that is not God's best for you, and you turn your back on the Lord's will to please this person, you will either watch them slip away from you no matter what you do, or what is sweet between you now will eventually become sour. Even when we are in God's perfect will relationship-wise, we will face disappointment regularly. So why would we want to be involved with a relationship that wasn't God's best for us? If our confidence and hope are properly placed in God, *He* will fulfill all our needs and desires.

Even when the Lord uses others to meet some of our needs, we are not to become dependent upon these people or place our confidence in them. While we should appreciate them, we should depend upon God only. Some believers compromise their Christian values because they're afraid of being alone. But those fears are unfounded because God has promised to provide *all* our needs if we let Him, and that includes our social and emotional needs. Jesus knew better than anyone what it was like to be disappointed and alone. Just before He went to the cross He said to His disciples, "You will leave me all alone. Yet I am not alone, for my Father is with me" (John 16:32). Jesus knew that even if all His loved ones deserted Him, His Father would still be

LIVE ON PURPOSE TODAY

What expectations are you waiting on? How are you going to feel if they fall through? Before this happens, decide now that no matter the outcome, you will trust God. Verbally announce to God your trust in Him. Commit to avoiding disappointment by only placing your trust in God rather than in man.

there for Him. That's a message for all of us to take to heart. It's my prayer that today you'll put your whole trust in the only One who could ever truthfully say, "I will never, never fail you nor forsake you"! (Heb. 13:5 TLB).

PRAYER

Lord, right now I commit myself to You and ask You to bring me into the center of Your will in every area of my life. Don't let me compromise my relationship with You to please myself or others. When others disappoint me, I ask that You comfort me and remind me that Your presence and provision are always available to me. Thank You that because my hope is in You, I won't be disappointed!

Who Needs Signs?

> *While the harpist was playing, the hand of the Lord*
> *came upon Elisha and he said, "This is what the Lord says:*
> *Make this valley full of ditches. For this is what the Lord says:*
> *You will see neither wind nor rain, yet this valley will be filled*
> *with water, and you, your cattle and your other animals will*
> *drink. This is an easy thing in the eyes of the Lord...."*
>
> 2 KINGS 3:16-18

The kings of Israel, Judah, and Edom had united to attack Moab. After a seven-day march, the army had no water left for themselves or their animals. Their situation looked hopeless, and they were prepared to die. Then good King Jehoshaphat summoned Elisha, the prophet of God, who revealed the Lord's plan to perform a miracle on their behalf. To me, the most amazing part of this prophecy is the Lord saying, "You will see neither wind nor rain...." God is saying here, "You're not going to see any signs that a miracle is coming, but it's coming just the same." And not only was God going to do something that was virtually impossible, but He said, "This is an *easy* thing in the eyes of the Lord"!

I can think of so many times that I encountered challenges in my life—and though a part of me hoped God would intervene on my behalf—my faith faltered because I thought, *I don't see any signs that He's doing anything!* Are you waiting to see some evidence that God is working on your behalf in a situation? Are you waiting for the right phone call, letter in the mail, or other tangible evidence?

Rest assured that it is an easy thing for God to come to your aid, even when signs that He will do so are virtually nonexistent!

PRAYER

Lord, forgive me when I've doubted You because I couldn't see any signs that You had plans to help me.

Remind me that Your power and wisdom transcend my comprehension, and that Your love for me knows no bounds. Thank You that my deliverance is on its way—with or without signs!

LIVE ON PURPOSE TODAY

Believing that your deliverance is on the way with or without signs, lift your hands toward heaven and thank God for His goodness, for His mercy that endures forever, and for His mighty power at work in your behalf!

Choosing God's Best

{ *Where is the man who fears the Lord?*
God will teach him how to choose the best. }

PSALM 25:12 TLB

I have a sister who is unemployed right now. She's single and she has a new home, so she's understandably concerned about her situation. The other day she got an offer for a job in her field. Even though she sensed that she would be "settling" if she accepted this position, she felt obligated to go on the interview because she was in desperate need of employment. Going on the interview only convinced her even more that it was not God's best for her. I told her not to feel badly about not wanting the job, and I suggested that the Lord only sent this opportunity her way to encourage her heart. After all, she and I had been earnestly praying that God would send her some special encouragement, and perhaps that's all this job offer was meant to be. I told her that when my husband, Joe, was out of work a couple of years ago, he was most discouraged when he wasn't getting a single "lead." When he did get a lead now and then, it encouraged him greatly, because it reminded him that God had not forgotten him and that He was indeed working on his behalf. I also pointed out to my sister that we can learn a lot from job interviews, and they can help us realize what we really want in a job and what we don't. I always take great comfort in the fact that the Lord knows us better than we know ourselves, and He alone knows what we *really* want—we don't. I've gotten to the point now where I ask God for something, but I also make it clear to Him that if it's not

His best for me, then I don't want it. Praying like this is still hard on my "flesh." But I'm learning more and more that God really does know best, and He will help us to receive His best in every situation if we will pray, do our part, and wait on Him for His perfect will and timing. Psalm 25:12 TLB says, "Where is the man who fears the Lord? God will teach him how to choose the best." Those who approach God with an attitude of trust and obedience will find that He is more than willing to help them choose His best every time.

LIVE ON PURPOSE TODAY

Are you settling in some areas of your life even though you know that God desires better for you? Stop wavering and choose God's best for your life. If it means utilizing self-control and abstaining from pleasures, have faith that God's best far exceeds quick satisfaction.

When you're waiting upon God for something to come to pass, ask Him to send some special encouragement your way. But when He does, remember to keep praying and standing in faith for His very best!

PRAYER

Lord, Your Word says, "A man's mind plans his way, but the Lord directs his steps and makes them sure" (Prov. 16:9 AMP). Therefore, I pray that no matter what my mind plans—no matter what anyone else plans for me—that You, Lord, would direct my steps and make them sure. Send me some encouragement while I'm waiting on You, but don't let me settle for less than Your best!

God-Pleasers Vs. Man-Pleasers

Am I now trying to win the approval of men, or of God?
Or am I trying to please men? If I were still trying
to please men, I would not be a servant of Christ.

GALATIANS 1:10

T he above verse, written by the apostle Paul, warns us that if we are to be true servants of God, we must seek the Lord's approval, rather than man's. Very often God's will and man's are opposed to each other, and here's where the tension arises. Jesus said, "What is highly valued among men is detestable in God's sight" (Luke 16:15). God and man have very different value systems, and we are expected to make right choices, even in tough situations. In Luke 12:48, Jesus tells us, "From everyone who has been given much, much will be demanded; and from the one who has been entrusted with much, much more will be asked." As children of God, we are equipped with the power of the Holy Spirit to live by God's standards, not the world's. The Bible assures us that our God is a just God, and He will never give us unattainable goals to strive for. When we supply the will, He supplies the power. Exodus 23:2 says, "Do not follow the crowd in doing wrong." Jesus said, "Unless you are faithful in small matters, you won't be faithful in large ones" (Luke 16:10 NLT). Don't be deceived into thinking that God doesn't care about the little details of our daily lives. He cares very much, and He expects us to be faithful. Proverbs 25:26 says, "If the godly compromise with the wicked, it is like polluting a fountain or muddying a spring." Not only can our compromise harm our fellowship with God, but it can damage our witness and cost us an opportunity to lead others to the Lord. It's been said that, "People may doubt what you say, but they will believe what you do." Instead of just telling them about Jesus, we need to show them Jesus! We're always appalled when we hear the biblical account of Peter denying Jesus. But look what the apostle Paul says in Titus 1:16: "They claim to know God, but by their actions they deny him." We're no better than Peter when we choose to live our own way, rather than God's. The Bible says that "friendship with the world is hatred toward God" (James 4:4). God's not going to settle for a superficial commitment from us. We have a higher calling on our lives, and it's the Lord's desire to use us for His glory. But He can't use us if we won't submit to His ways and plans for us. In 1 Timothy 1:12, Paul says, "I thank Christ Jesus our Lord, who has given me strength, that he considered me faithful, appointing me to his service." God has promised to reward our faithfulness by giving us opportunities to serve Him. But there are other rewards for choosing to please God rather than people. When we make it our life's goal to please the Lord, the result is joy, peace, and fulfillment. On the other hand, whenever we try to please other people, we experience frustration, disappointment, and emptiness. The truth is that living to please God is the only decent way to live. My prayer for you today is that you will have the same spirit

LIVE ON PURPOSE TODAY

No one can answer these questions better than you: Do you claim to know God but deny Him with your actions? Do you work to please men more than God? If you answered yes, purpose that today is a day of change!

that Peter and the other disciples did when they declared, "We must obey God rather than men"! (Acts 5:29).

PRAYER

*Lord, forgive me for the times I chose to please
other people instead of You. Give me the strength and
courage I need to resist the temptation to win the approval
of others. Help me to be faithful in little things so that You can
trust me to be faithful in bigger ones. Thank You for rewarding
my faithfulness with wonderful opportunities to serve You!*

Unwholesome Talk

"Do not let any unwholesome talk come out of your mouths,
but only what is helpful for building others up according
to their needs, that it may benefit those who listen.
And do not grieve the Holy Spirit of God, with
whom you were sealed for the day of redemption."

EPHESIANS 4:29,30

I recently heard from a young man who wanted to know what the Bible had to say about using profane language. He said that he had a friend who cursed constantly. When he told his friend that it was a sin against God and that he wanted him to stop, the friend said that he would, if it could be proven that Scripture clearly condemned it. I was more than happy to provide this young man with numerous verses from the Bible that supported his claim.

Hearing from this young man reminded me of an experience I had when I was in high school many years ago. I was sitting on the school bus with one of my best friends, when she began spouting a stream of obscenities. I was stunned, and I promptly informed her that cursing was a sin. She then reassured me that it was not a sin, but only using the Lord's name in vain was sinful. At the time it didn't even occur to me to search the Bible to see if my friend was right. Her explanation sounded logical to me, and it wasn't long before I began using some profane words myself. As I look back on this experience, I realize that it was the perfect example of why Christians need to have a working knowledge of the Bible. If we don't, we will not be able to discern truth from error. Jesus Himself said, "Your error is caused by your ignorance of the Scriptures" (Matt. 22:29 TLB). And the apostle Paul wrote, "Find out what pleases the Lord" (Eph. 5:10), and, "Know what His word says and means" (2 Tim. 2:15 TLB).

Paul also wrote, "But among you there must not be even a hint of sexual immorality, or of any kind of impurity, or of greed, because these are improper for God's holy people. Nor should there be obscenity, foolish talk or coarse joking, which are out of place, but rather thanksgiving" (Eph. 5:3,4). Paul never minced words. He makes it abundantly clear that God holds His children to a higher standard than the world, and He expects our speech to reflect our commitment to Him and to holiness. Paul says again in Colossians 3:8, "But now you must rid yourselves of all such things as these: anger, rage, malice, slander, and filthy language from your lips." When you know that someone is a Christian and you hear them curse or tell a dirty joke, how do you view them? Do you think their coarse language hurts their witness? You bet it does. The devil delights in trying to make believers think that their speech doesn't matter to God, or that it has no bearing on their Christian witness. It's time that God's people wake up and realize that their sloppy language is not a small thing in the Lord's sight, but that He takes it very seriously.

LIVE ON PURPOSE TODAY

If your words are less desirable than what God expects from you, take steps to change your vocabulary. Confess Psalm 19:12 every day and ask God to help you speak only words that line up with His Word.

Jesus said, "But I tell you that men will have to give account on the day of judgment for every careless word they have spoken. For by your words you will be acquitted, and by your words you will be condemned" (Matt. 12:36,37). Every word that comes out of our mouths is important to God. And when our speech isn't pleasing to the Lord, we grieve His heart. Paul wrote, "Don't use foul or abusive language. Let everything you say be good and helpful, so that your words will be an encouragement to those who hear them. And do not bring sorrow to God's Holy Spirit by the way you live" (Eph. 4:29,30 NLT). God gave us the power of speech so that we would use it to glorify Him and edify others.

My prayer for you today is that you will get serious about the words you allow to come out of your mouth, and that you will continually pray as David did—"May the words of my mouth and the thoughts of my heart be pleasing to You, O Lord, my Rock and my Redeemer"! (Ps. 19:12 NLT).

PRAYER

Lord, forgive me for sloppy speech that may have harmed others or caused them to doubt Your presence in me. Give me a holy fear of You and Your commands so that I may always please You with my language and my life. Thank You that as I devote myself to You and Your Word, I will touch and change lives for Your glory!

Don't Look Back—or Ahead

> *Therefore, do not worry about tomorrow, for tomorrow will worry about itself. Each day has enough trouble of its own.*
>
> MATTHEW 6:34

Jesus makes it clear here that He doesn't want us worrying about the future. A certain amount of planning is okay, as long as it's done with God's wisdom and guidance. But worrying is another story. It's not only nonproductive, but it can be destructive, too. When Jesus prayed the Lord's Prayer for His disciples, He said, "Give us this day our daily bread." Notice He didn't ask for enough bread for a year, a month, or even a week. When the children of Israel were in the desert those forty years, God provided manna for them daily. But He gave them strict orders to gather only what they needed for that day. If they attempted to gather more, it would decay. God wants to be our Provider, and He wants us to depend on His care and provision daily.

These principles don't just apply to our material needs, but to our spiritual needs as well. If you belong to the Lord and you depend on His grace to live each day, you have only the grace you need for today, whatever it may bring. You don't have the grace to live in the past. And you don't have the grace to live in the future. That's why when you live in the past, you will suffer regret and torment. And if you live in the future, you will be plagued with anxiety and fear. Eventually, your mind and body will pay the price. But if you live each day depending on God and His provision and grace, you will experience an inner peace and joy, no matter what the circumstances. Instead of looking ahead or behind, look up into the blessed face of the Savior—and He will make your cup overflow!

PRAYER

Lord, help me not to live in the past or worry about tomorrow. Give me the grace I need each day to face all my responsibilities and challenges with confidence and courage. Teach me how to depend on You and trust in You so that I'll never have to be fearful of what the future may bring. Thank You that You're all I'll ever need!

LIVE ON PURPOSE TODAY

Determine to keep yourself in "today"! If you catch yourself harboring regrets, you've slipped into yesterday. If you catch yourself in anxiety, you've leaped into tomorrow. Anchor yourself to God's Word where there's plenty of grace for *today*.

The Positive Power of Saying "No"

Since Jesus went through everything you're going through and more, learn to think like him. Think of your sufferings as a weaning from that old sinful habit of always expecting to get your own way. Then you'll be able to live out your days free to pursue what God wants instead of being tyrannized by what you want.

1 PETER 4:1,2 MESSAGE

I recently read about a minister of the Gospel whose grateful congregation had sent him on a cruise. During his trip he made the discovery that indulging his appetite had let it get totally out of control. I believe that reading about this man's experience was God's way of confirming that I was on the right track with my new eating habits. After having tried some popular diets that allowed the dieter to eat small quantities of anything they wanted—and after achieving dismal results—the Lord began instructing me to say "no" to many of my own natural desires, and to say "yes" to wiser ones. I discovered that the more I resisted having my own way where my eating was concerned, the more control I gained over my appetite. This control enabled me to not only lose weight, but to keep it off, as well.

The verses above from The Message Bible were life-changing for me. They made me realize how doing what I feel like doing all the time allows my natural desires to bully me. The more I give in to myself, the harder it becomes to discipline myself to do the right thing. On the other hand, the more I resist my natural impulses to indulge myself, the more control and freedom I gain—which is what God wants for His children. For instance, often when I go shopping and get the impulse to buy something, I begin to feel a "tension" between my flesh and my spirit. My flesh may say, "You can't pass this up—it's on sale!" But my spirit will give me a "check" about it, warning me to resist the urge to buy it. Then I have to decide which I want to please more—my spirit or my flesh. Either way, I will have to endure some kind of suffering. If I say "no" to myself, my flesh will suffer. If I say "yes" to myself, my spirit will suffer. I've discovered that if I can't get out of a situation without suffering somehow, it's best if I suffer in my flesh, rather than in my spirit. That's the attitude Jesus had, and that's what the verses above are referring to. The Living Bible puts it this way: "Since Christ suffered and underwent pain, you must have the same attitude he did; you must be ready to suffer, too. For remember, when your body suffers, sin loses its power, and you won't be

LIVE ON PURPOSE TODAY

Where have you been saying "yes," when you should have been saying "no"? When you have the answer to that question, find Scriptures that strengthen your "no," and remain steadfast in their support.

spending the rest of your life chasing after evil desires, but will be anxious to do the will of God" (1 Peter 4:1,2 TLB). Every time we choose to suffer in our flesh rather than have our own way, sin's hold over us diminishes and it becomes easier to obey God. Before we accepted Christ as our Savior, there was no way we could have escaped the enslavement of sin. But with the gift of salvation comes the gift of the Holy Spirit, and the power to live a godly life in a fleshly body and a sinful world. God doesn't give us His Spirit just so we can live like the rest of the world. He gives us supernatural power so that we can say "no" to sin and live the abundant life that Jesus died to give us. Can we quench the Spirit's power working in us? Absolutely. If we continually ignore the Holy Spirit's conviction and leading, our hearts can become hardened and it can become increasingly difficult to hear God's "still, small voice." First Peter 1:14 in The Message Bible says, "Don't lazily slip back into those old grooves of evil, doing just what you feel like doing. You didn't know any better then; you do now." The truth is, you don't have to give in to your sinful nature anymore when it makes demands on you. The Bible says that you've been given a new nature (2 Cor. 5:17), and if you'll live your life with an attitude of total dependence upon God, you can enjoy the freedom that's found in doing His will. Don't let anyone tell you that doing what you feel like doing all the time will make you happy. The fact is that it will make you miserable. If you really want to enjoy your life and receive all the blessings God has for you, begin today to give yourself lots of daily doses of "No"!

PRAYER

Lord, when I'm tempted to have my own way against Your will, remind me of how my indulgence could harm my health, my finances, or my relationship with You or others. Help me to live a disciplined lifestyle so I can receive Your best in every area of my life. Thank You for the control and freedom that saying "no" to myself will bring!

Avoiding Entanglement

I am sending you out like sheep among wolves.
Therefore be as shrewd as snakes and as innocent as doves.

MATTHEW 10:16

I recently heard from a young man who was doing his best to minister to a nonbeliever over the Internet. He sent me a copy of one of her recent e-mails, and it immediately became clear to me that this girl had some serious mental and emotional problems. This young man asked me what I would do if I were in his situation, trying to help this girl and lead her to the Lord. When I wrote him back, I told him frankly that I would keep a healthy distance from someone who is so obviously disturbed, and who is destructive to herself and others. I urged him to pray for wisdom and discernment so that he would know what God's will was concerning his relationship with this girl. I advised him to earnestly pray for her salvation and deliverance, and to begin distancing himself from her, with God's help. I explained to him that very few of us are equipped to handle the kinds of problems that this girl was dealing with, and that it would be wiser for him to pray that the Lord would send her the proper help and that she would be receptive to it.

Perhaps my response to this young man seems cold and unfeeling to you. I might have thought so, too, a few years ago. But after seeing so many well-meaning Christians fall into sin and despair in situations like these, I've changed my view. While the Lord often calls us to minister to troubled people, it is never His will for us to become "entangled" with them or their problems. Some Christians mistakenly believe that they can minister to people over the Internet without fear of getting too involved. They have a false sense of security, thinking that they are "safe" from the harm that a destructive relationship can cause. As servants of God we need to have better spiritual discernment than that. The truth is that Satan often uses people like this disturbed girl to distract believers, not only from their God-given purpose, but from the day-to-day plans that the Lord has laid out for them. If the devil can keep us busy trying to help one or two troubled people, our effectiveness as ministers of the Gospel will be severely limited. I have seen some Christians spending a lot of time and energy trying to help people who don't even appreciate their help, or who have no intention of changing their course of destruction. Troubled people like these will drain the life out of us. They are more likely to drag us down than we are to lift them up. These folks need much more than a supportive friend—they need a Savior. And that's a role reserved for Christ alone, and one that none of us can fill, no matter how we try. I warned this young man that as long as he persisted in his efforts to keep this troubled girl propped up, she might never realize her need for God. Unfortunately, people like her often need to hit bottom before they acknowledge their need for a Savior. When that's the case, those of

LIVE ON PURPOSE TODAY

Is there someone that *pulls from* you more than they *pour into* you? Ask the Lord to reveal whether or not this relationship is "toxic" in your life. If so, begin to take steps away from this person and direct them towards someone more qualified to help them.

us who try to keep these people afloat may actually be hindering the work that God wants to do in their lives.

Jesus told His disciples, "I am sending you out like sheep among wolves. Therefore be as shrewd as snakes and as innocent as doves" (Matt. 10:16). The Lord is talking about a delicate balance here. He doesn't want us being deceitful or malicious. But He also doesn't want us being naive or gullible. While we don't want to go through life with suspicious minds, we also don't want to be so unsuspecting that we become totally useless to God. Jesus commanded us to, "Be on guard against men" (Matt. 10:17), and that's a warning that we should take seriously. Today, if you are in a situation like this young man was, I urge you to earnestly seek the Lord about it. It's my heartfelt prayer that every one of your relationships would be *all* that God wants them to be, and *only* what He wants them to be!

PRAYER

Lord, Your Word says, "A prudent man sees danger and takes refuge, but the simple keep going and suffer for it" (Prov. 22:3). Therefore, I ask that You make me wise and discerning where all of my relationships are concerned so that I will not have to suffer the consequences of being involved in destructive relationships. Help me to always be ready and willing to minister to others, but keep me from spending more time or energy in these efforts than is Your will for me. Thank You, Lord, that with Your help, my relationships will always please and glorify You!

Grace for the Guilty

"Now the king of Aram had ordered his chariot commanders, "Do not fight with anyone, small or great, except the king of Israel." When the chariot commanders saw Jehoshaphat, they thought, "This is the king of Israel." So they turned to attack him, but Jehoshaphat cried out, and the Lord helped him.

2 CHRONICLES 18:30,31

King Jehoshaphat was king of Judah, and he had a heart for God. But he unwisely made an alliance with evil King Ahab of Israel. When their armies attacked the Arameans, Ahab shrewdly disguised himself, while insisting that Jehoshaphat wear his royal robes. Consequently, the Arameans—who were ordered to kill only the king of Israel—mistook Jehoshaphat for Ahab, and they tried to kill him. Jehoshaphat cried out to the Lord, who saved His servant from destruction.

This message is good news today for those of us who have a heart for God but sometimes miss the mark. Are you in financial trouble today because of poor planning or foolish spending? Did you get involved in a relationship that was out of God's will for you? Are you overweight today because of poor eating habits? Maybe you've adopted the attitude, "I've made my bed, now I'll have to lie in it." You may feel like you deserve to suffer the consequences of your mistake, and you don't even feel like you can ask God for help. Jehoshaphat made a terrible mistake, but when faced with the consequences of his actions, he cried out to God and was rescued. No matter how great your sin, turn to the Lord today and receive His mercy and grace. In John chapter 9 of The Message Bible, Jesus speaks some words which I pray will be a comfort to you: "You're looking for someone to blame.... Look instead for what God can do"!

LIVE ON PURPOSE TODAY

Do you feel that you've missed the mark in some way? It's so important to look instead at what God can do! Search God's Word today for Scriptures that will infuse you with strength to forge a better path.

PRAYER

Lord, sometimes I feel so guilty when I know I've done wrong that it's difficult for me to seek You afterwards. The next time I fail You, help me to turn to You right away for forgiveness and help. Please don't let my guilt or pride come between us. Give me a pure heart and a steadfast spirit. Thank You for Your promise to continue the work You've begun in me!

Boosting Our Prayer Power

And receive from Him anything we ask, because
we obey His commands and do what pleases Him.

1 JOHN 3:22

This Scripture reveals an important biblical principle—the power of our prayers is directly related to our obedience to God's Word and to our desire to do what pleases Him. As we progress in our level of obedience to the Lord, the effectiveness of our prayers will increase. Proverbs 28:9 says, "If anyone turns a deaf ear to the law, even his prayers are detestable." This is another verse that shows a connection between our obedience and our prayers. Even though we've made a decision to trust Christ as our Savior, we can't expect ready answers to our prayers when we ignore God's commands. Psalm 66:18-19 says, "If I had cherished sin in my heart, the Lord would not have listened; but God has surely listened and heard my voice in prayer." If we want God to honor our prayers, we can't wink at sin or have unconfessed sin in our lives. We also can't afford to harbor unforgiveness toward anyone. Jesus made that clear when He was teaching us how to have mountain-moving faith in Mark 11: "And when you stand praying, if you hold anything against anyone, forgive him, so that your Father in heaven may forgive you your sins" (v. 25). The Bible reveals that the quality of our relationships can determine the effectiveness of our prayers. Peter says that husbands must "be considerate" of their wives and "treat them with respect" so that their "prayers may not be hindered" (1 Peter 3:7). This principle applies to our other relationships, as well.

Jesus said, "If you abide in Me, and My words abide in you, ask whatever you wish, and it shall be done for you" (John 15:7 NASB). The Lord is promising us here that if we will live for Him and obey

His Word, He will hear and answer our prayers. If you have unsaved or backslidden loved ones, your prayers can make all the difference in their lives. Job 22:30 says, "He will deliver even one who is not innocent, who will be delivered through the cleanness of your hands." Our prayers of intercession can be especially powerful when we are fully committed to the

LIVE ON PURPOSE TODAY

What has God told you to do that you are not doing? Are you serious about boosting your prayer power? Then put your actions in line with your commitment. Today, make the decision to do whatever God has told you to do. Don't wait another minute!

Lord. This is particularly important when we are unable to reach our loved ones with our conversation or example. Our prayers can be our best "secret weapon" in winning them to Christ. Scripture admonishes us to "find out what pleases the Lord" (Eph. 5:10). If we will do our part in committing ourselves to learning and doing God's will, the Lord will do His part in blessing us and honoring our prayers. And God doesn't expect us to do it on our own. Philippians 2:13 TLB promises, "God is at work within you, helping you want to obey him, and then helping you do what he wants." And we can pray like David did, "Teach me to do your will, for you are my God; may your good Spirit lead me on level ground" (Ps. 143:10). Start getting serious about obeying God, and start boosting your prayer power today!

PRAYER

Lord, forgive me for the times I haven't taken my prayer responsibilities seriously. Remind me that my prayers can bring salvation to the lost, healing to the sick, and deliverance to those in trouble. Give me the grace and the desire to do Your will in everything. Thank You that as I sow seeds of obedience, I'll reap an abundance of answered prayer!

You Can't Please People

I, even I, am He who comforts you and gives you all this joy.
So what right have you to fear mere mortal men,
who wither like the grass and disappear?
And yet you have no fear of God, your Maker—you have
forgotten Him, the one who spread the stars throughout the
skies and made the earth. Will you be in constant dread
of man's oppression, and fear their anger all day long?

ISAIAH 51:12,13 TLB

I've lived long enough to have discovered a very important fact of life—you can't please people. One of the things I love most about serving God and living for Him is that I no longer have to live in fear of people's disapproval. All I have to do is concentrate on pleasing God, who never changes, and I'll succeed in life. It's a freedom that I appreciate and can't live without. I began experiencing this freedom for myself when I started studying the Bible and discovering what God says about trying to be a people pleaser. Proverbs 29:25 NLT says, "Fearing people is a dangerous trap, but to trust the Lord means safety." Trying to win the approval of people can lead to disappointment, frustration, and emptiness. But seeking God's approval brings peace, contentment, and fulfillment. Those who strive to please others are often unstable. You can't count on them, and neither can God. They are often easily intimidated, and they can be talked into or out of something, even though their own hearts condemn them for it. The Bible says, "Do not fear their intimidation, and do not be troubled" (1 Peter 3:14 NASB). Right before Jesus' departure, He leaves

His disciples His perfect peace and tells them, "Do not permit yourselves to be fearful and intimidated and cowardly and unsettled" (John 14:27 AMP). Trying to please people will rob us of our peace, and because of that, it can harm our mental, emotional, and physical health. On the other hand, "The fear of the Lord leads to life: Then one rests content, untouched by trouble" (Prov. 19:23).

The good news is that we can depend on God all the time. He tells us in His Word, "I the Lord do not change" (Mal. 3:6). And James tells us that our God "does not change like shifting shadows" (James 1:17). Can you imagine if people recorded their own laws? They would have to be altered continually to keep up with our tendency to change the rules as we go along. But God won't ever change, and neither will His Word. God wants to bless us and use us for His glory, but He can't do that if we're busy trying to please others, instead of seeking His perfect will for our lives each day. The Bible says, "All who are led by the Spirit of God are children of God" (Rom. 8:14 NLT). It's God's will for us to be Spirit-led, not people-led. Otherwise, God will not be able to count on us, and He will have to put us on a shelf instead of using us to make a real difference in this world. The apostle Paul was a great example of a God

LIVE ON PURPOSE TODAY

Do you invest more time in trying to please others instead of spending time acting on God's directives for your life? Don't put off what God is asking you to do. If you are more concerned with pleasing others instead of God, you will be disappointed down the road. Choose God's way, even if it results in less recognition from man.

pleaser, and the Lord used Him mightily. In Galatians 1:10 NLT, Paul exclaims, "Obviously, I'm not trying to be a people pleaser! No, I'm trying to please God. If I were trying to please people, I would not be Christ's servant." If we want to be true servants of Christ, we're going to have to actively seek God daily, ask for His guidance, and then yield to the promptings of His Spirit. Sometimes what people want us to do and what God wants us to do will be the same, but many times they will conflict. It's up to us to choose whom we will obey. If you are in the habit of trying to please people, remember this—it can't be done. My prayer for you today is that in everything, you'll set your heart on pleasing God and discover for yourself the peace and freedom that only He can give!

PRAYER

Lord, help me to seek Your perfect will in everything each day. Teach me to be sensitive and obedient to the promptings of Your Spirit. Guard me from the fear of man, and grant me a holy fear and reverence for You. Thank You for the peace, joy, and freedom I'll enjoy as a result!

Pursuing Peace in Our Families

Without wood a fire goes out;
without gossip a quarrel dies down.

PROVERBS 26:20

T his Scripture not only changed my life, it changed my entire family. I was raised in an environment where criticism and sarcasm were prevalent, even though my parents loved me and my sisters very much. By the time I discovered this Scripture several years ago, decades of grudges, gripes, and ill feelings had accumulated. My siblings and I had children of our own, and three generations in my family had learned to live with strife and dissension. Once I became a committed Christian, I became increasingly uncomfortable with the gossip and sarcasm. God showed me the above verse and made it clear to me that I would have to take the initiative to bring about change in my family. The Living Bible version of this verse says, "Fire goes out for lack of fuel, and tensions disappear when gossip stops." Every time one of my relatives criticized or slandered someone else in my family and I joined in, I was adding fuel to the fire that was destroying the peace and harmony of my household. God instructed me to stop adding to the strife in my family by refusing to participate in any malicious talk against my relatives. When I was personally attacked or criticized, the Lord helped me to quickly forgive the offender and to resist responding with a hurtful retort. It wasn't easy and the change didn't happen overnight, but my obedience brought about a healing in my entire family that established a peace, unity, and harmony that is an awesome testimony to the power and truth of God's Word.

If you're tired of the strife in your family and you want it to change, I can tell you from experience that you can make a difference. But you've got to be committed, and you've got to rely on God's grace, because the devil isn't going to make it easy for you. Satan is determined to create strife and division in our families because he knows that the fullness of God's blessings are bestowed upon those who dwell in unity and harmony. (Ps. 133:1,3.) He also knows that "a home filled with argument and strife is doomed" (Luke 11:17 TLB). But if you are a child of God, you are equipped with Holy Spirit power to overcome the enemy's schemes. The Bible tells us to "work hard at living in peace with others" (Ps. 34:14; 1 Peter 3:11 NLT). If you're serious about wanting peace in your family, you're going to have to work hard at it. You're going to have to "make allowance for each other's faults and forgive the person who offends you." If you can't do it for any other reason, then do it simply because "the Lord forgave you" (Col. 3:13 NLT). When it's absolutely necessary to confront a family member about their behavior, don't talk about them behind their back, but "speak the

LIVE ON PURPOSE TODAY

Have you spoken words over your family that are sarcastic or demeaning? Start fresh today by speaking one sentence of encouragement over each of them. Do not let the sun go down without speaking words of life over your friends and family today.

truth in love" (Eph. 4:15). Make an effort to speak only words that encourage, build up, and benefit others. (Eph. 4:29.) And pray for your family. Your prayers can move the mighty hand of God in awesome ways. Rest assured that the Lord will honor you for your faithfulness, obedience, and love. My prayer for you is that today you'll take the first step toward bringing healing to your household and discover for yourself the heavenly rewards of a family dwelling in peace!

PRAYER

Lord, give me a holy determination to initiate healing in my household, and show me how to take the first step. When I'm tempted to participate in behavior that produces strife, remind me that I have the Holy Spirit power to make a difference. Make me quick to forgive and help me to always speak the truth in love. Thank You for blessing my family with peace and harmony as a result!

Praise in the Midst of Problems

Sometimes when I'm going through a trial, I have a tendency to wear myself out trying to gain the victory. I pray almost constantly, I study my Bible with zeal, and I meditate on God's Word day and night. These are all good things that please the Lord, but I know from experience that it's possible to carry them to extremes. This was the case recently for me when God had to remind me that real faith ushers us into the rest of God. (Heb. 4:3.) After impressing upon me that I was actually doing more fretting than resting, He spoke to my heart and said, "Just praise Me." At first, I had to do it by faith because my troubles had plunged me deep into a pit of depression. As I began to sing praises to the Lord, I felt my spirits lift and my focus shift from my problems to the Problem Solver. And that was exactly what I needed because when I'm going through a trial, I have a tendency to want to figure out how I can get out of it. Unfortunately, this doesn't do a thing to bolster my faith, but instead it just adds to my doubt, confusion, and frustration. King Jehoshaphat had the right attitude when a "vast army" came against him and his people in 2 Chronicles 20. He knew the odds were stacked against him and there was no apparent way out of his trouble. He turned to the Lord and told Him, "We do not know what to do, but our eyes are upon You" (2 Chron. 20:12). God brought this passage to my remembrance when I was up against my own vast army, and He showed me how singing praises to Him would help me to keep my eyes on Him instead of my circumstances. I realized then that I didn't need to know *how* the Lord would deliver me—only that He would. And along with this realization came the peace, joy, and reassurance that I so desperately needed.

The Bible says that David was a man after God's own heart. (Acts 13:22.) One reason for that was his willingness to praise God in the darkest of times. Scripture reveals that after his first child with Bathsheba died, he went straight to the temple to worship the Lord. (2 Sam. 12:20.) David knew that no matter what was going on in his life, God was still worthy of his devotion and praise. In Psalm 34:1, he writes, "I will bless the Lord at all times; His praise shall continually be in my mouth." I especially like the way the Living Bible puts it: "I will praise the Lord no matter what happens." And even though David was a mighty warrior who often relied on weapons of war for his defense, he also knew that praise was an important weapon in his arsenal. In Psalm 18:3, he writes, "I will call upon the Lord, who is worthy to be praised, so shall I be saved from my enemies." If you are going through some difficult times right now,

LIVE ON PURPOSE TODAY

Praising God can be a life-changing act. Buy a good praise and worship CD and begin praising God as you drive to work or while you are working around the house. Allow the words to sink into your mind and spirit. Before you know it, you will be singing praises unto God throughout your day.

don't despair. Begin right now to sing praises to the Lord and discover for yourself the peace, joy, and victory that a praise-filled heart can bring!

PRAYER

Lord, teach me how to praise You continually, even in the midst of adversity. Show me how to shift my focus from myself and my problems to You. Remind me that even when the odds are stacked against me, You have a perfect plan for my deliverance. Thank You, Lord, that as I praise You in the midst of my problems, I will be blessed and You will be glorified!

God's Perfect Timing

For the vision is yet for an appointed time and it hastens
to the end [fulfillment]; it will not deceive or disappoint.
Though it tarry, wait [earnestly] for it, because it will surely
come; it will not be behindhand on its appointed day.

HABAKKUK 2:3 AMP

Almost two years ago my husband, Joe, applied for a job in the company where his friend and former coworker, Rob, was employed. My husband really wanted and needed this position. Even so, we put this job "on the altar," and we asked the Lord to close every door if it wasn't His best for Joe. My husband's interview went so well that Rob told him that the job was his. Nevertheless, doors began closing against Joe, and the job was given to someone else. Even though we were disappointed, we tried to take comfort in the knowledge that the Lord had intervened in order to keep my husband in His perfect will.

Recently, Rob approached Joe with a second opportunity for them to work together. A job which was almost identical to the one that my husband lost had opened up, and though Joe was hesitant to try a second time, Rob convinced him that it was worth a shot. Once again, even though we really wanted this job for Joe, we prayed that God would open and close the right doors so that my husband would be kept in the Lord's perfect will. We were all amazed when every door that seemed closed the first time opened wide. Joe was offered the job, and he accepted.

What made the difference between these two experiences? God's timing. In both instances my family and I prayed the same way. We asked the Lord to open and close the right doors so that my husband would be in His perfect will at all times. The first time, God closed doors. The second time, He opened them. As we earnestly sought the Lord's wisdom and guidance, He moved mightily to keep us in His will and timing.

There are times when it appears that God is saying "no" to us, but He's actually saying "wait." The Bible often uses phrases like "the appointed time" or "the proper time." Solomon wrote, "There is a proper time and procedure for every matter" (Eccl. 8:6). Ours is not a "hit-or-miss" God. He created us with specific plans and purposes in mind, and His timing is always perfect. Scripture says, "But these things I plan won't happen right away. Slowly, steadily, surely, the time approaches when the vision will be fulfilled. If it seems slow, do not despair, for these things will surely come to pass. Just be patient! They will not be overdue a single day!" (Hab. 2:3 TLB). As long as our trust is in God and we are praying and seeking Him daily, we can be sure that He is busy working behind the scenes to bring our God-given dreams and visions to pass. The

LIVE ON PURPOSE TODAY

Are you consumed with the future? Find three things about the present that you will miss once they have passed. It may be your toddler's crawling stage or precious moments with your aging parents. Whatever the present holds, savor it. The future will arrive soon enough in God's perfect timing.

Lord instructs us to be patient and not to despair, because He knows that impatience and discouragement can cause us to miss out on His best for us. Sometimes God makes us wait because certain circumstances are not yet right for us. Other times we're the ones who are not yet ready, or someone else involved is not prepared. As long as we are praying and believing God to work all things out for our good (Rom. 8:28), we can trust that He is actively working in our circumstances, in our lives, and in the lives of others. If you are waiting on God for some special blessing or breakthrough today, remember that delays are not necessarily denials. Keep your faith and hope in God, believing that at just the right time He will open doors for you. When He does, you will know without a doubt that it was worth the wait!

PRAYER

Lord, please teach me to always have an attitude that says, "God, if it's not Your will for me, I don't want it!" Help me to realize that even something that is Your will for me, but that is out of Your perfect timing, is still disobedience. Grant me the patience I need to wait upon You for Your absolute best. Thank You that as I keep in step with Your plans for me, my blessings won't be delayed a single day!

The Disaster of Wrong Desires

[They] did not wait for his counsel. In the desert they gave in to their craving; in the wasteland they put God to the test. So he gave them what they asked for, but sent a wasting disease upon them.

PSALM 106:13-15

Recently, my family and I had to make a decision about our pet situation. The wild mallards that we had hatched and raised with tender loving care had flown away to start a new life on their own. The joy that Sam and Lazarus had brought us was so abundant that their departure left a profound void in our daily routine. At first we were so saddened by our loss that getting another pet seemed unthinkable. But after my family and I talked and prayed about it, we began planning to acquire some new ducks. As we started making phone calls and combing the Internet looking for newborn ducklings, we discovered just how unlikely it would be for us to find them so late in the summer. It seemed that every time a new avenue opened up, we'd eventually encounter a dead end. My husband and I both began to suspect that it was not God's will for us to have the new pets we dreamed of. We entrusted the matter to the Lord, asking Him to help us do His will. From then on we became more cautious in our efforts, waiting upon God for direction. Shortly afterwards we got a call from a local farmer who had heard that we were in the market for pet ducklings. He invited us to drive out to his farm that evening to see if there were any in his flock that we would be interested in. As we headed home with our three new baby ducks that day, we praised and thanked God for His goodness and love.

When I was seeking God about getting new ducks, He showed me the verses above from Psalm 106. They tell of the Israelites' disobedience while they wandered in the desert after their escape from Egypt. When they demanded better food from the Lord, "He gave them what they asked for, but He sent a plague along with it" (Ps. 106:15 NLT). Verses 13 and 14 tell us why: "They did not wait for his counsel. In the desert they gave in to their craving...they put God to the test." Instead of waiting upon God to give them direction and to act in their best interests, the Israelites insisted on having their own way, testing God's patience and causing Him to send punishment along with the fulfillment of their demands. I had already been earnestly seeking God for His will in our pet situation, but after reading these verses I put my desires on the altar and offered them up to Him. I told the Lord that as much as I longed to have new ducks, I wanted no part of a plan that wasn't His best for us. I reaffirmed my trust in Him, as well as my belief that He always has our best interests at heart. I believe that by doing this I was giving

LIVE ON PURPOSE TODAY

The Bible promises that we can renew our mind by reading the Word. (Rom. 12:2.) Find one Scripture that will rewrite a wrong desire in your mind, memorize it, and speak it out loud. When the desire creeps into your mind, the Word of God will become your initial reaction to battle it. You will find that your desires will begin to line up with the Word of God instead of your flesh.

God the opportunity to close doors on my behalf, as well as open them. From then on I continued to follow any leads I felt the Lord might be offering, but I maintained a "ready mind" so that I'd be prepared to graciously accept His saying "no" to my desire for new pets. If you don't trust God and truly believe that He wants what is best for you, this strategy won't work for you and you'll wind up "kicking down doors" to get what you want. And you'll deeply regret it in the end. But if you truly believe the Lord when He promises to give you the desires of your heart if you'll delight yourself in Him (Ps. 37:4), you'll surrender your desires to God and trust Him to do what's best for you. My prayer for you today is that you'll put aside your wrong desires and choose God's will every time. When you do, you'll discover firsthand that those who put their hope in the Lord will never be disappointed! (Isa. 49:23.)

PRAYER

Lord, whenever I'm faced with decisions, help me to always wait upon Your direction. Remind me to give You the opportunity to close doors on my behalf, as well as open them. I pray that the desires of my heart will never be in conflict with the desires of Yours. Thank You for satisfying my desires with good things! (Ps. 103:5).

You Have a Job To Do

For we are God's workmanship, created in Christ Jesus to do good works, which God prepared in advance for us to do.

EPHESIANS 2:10

If you have received salvation through faith in Christ, then this verse applies to you and you need never again wonder if you were created for a purpose. You are God's masterpiece, re-created in Christ, to do good deeds and accomplish great things for God's glory. These acts and achievements were prepared by God in advance, before you were even born. You have a God-given purpose. If anyone tells you otherwise, they are dead wrong. Satan himself will try to convince you that you have no real purpose in life. He may even use other people to do it. But if you fall for that lie, you will live a meaningless, purposeless life. But you don't have to! Jeremiah 29:11 says, "For I know the plans I have for you," declares the Lord, "plans to prosper you and not to harm you, plans to give you hope and a future."

When Jesus told the Parable of the Talents, He was letting us know that each of us has a special purpose in life, and God expects us to cooperate with Him so that it is fulfilled. All three servants in the parable are given various talents, which represent the individual's gifts and resources. The servants who put their gifts to good use and were productive were rewarded by the master. They were given more resources and greater responsibility. But one of the servants was so fearful and self-centered that he buried his talent and was totally unfruitful for the master. Jesus

LIVE ON PURPOSE TODAY

God desires that none should perish from the life He has provided through His Son, Jesus. Ask God to provide an opportunity for you to share His love with another person. By doing this you are joining God in His plan for the world.

calls him a "worthless servant." If you are a child of God, He has blessed you with special gifts that He expects you to use for His glory. If you don't know what they are, ask Him to reveal them to you. Ephesians 5:15 AMP says that we should "live purposefully" and make the most of our time. You have a job to do! There may be people in this world right now who will never receive the gift of salvation unless you take your place in the body of Christ. It's my heartfelt prayer that you will make a decision today to cooperate with God's plan for your life and align your will with His. If you do, God's promise in Psalm 138:8 belongs to you: "The Lord will fulfill his purpose for me"!

PRAYER

Lord, today I commit to You all that I am and all that I have, and I ask that You fulfill Your purpose for my life. Show me what my gifts are and help me to use them for Your glory. Use me to lead others to You. The next time I doubt that my life has a special purpose, remind me of the truth. Thank You that You will fulfill Your purpose for me and that You will be glorified!

Persistence Pays Off

I have posted watchmen on your walls, O Jerusalem; they will never be silent day or night. You who call on the Lord, give yourselves no rest, and give him no rest till he establishes Jerusalem and makes her the praise of the earth.

ISAIAH 62:6,7

The value of persistent prayer is a recurrent theme throughout the Bible. In Luke chapter 11, right after the disciples ask Jesus to teach them to pray and He gifts them with the Lord's Prayer, He tells the parable about the man seeking three loaves of bread from a friend who is already in bed for the night. He concludes by stating that because of the man's persistence, his friend will relent and "give him as much as he needs" (v. 8). Then again in Luke chapter 18, Jesus tells them the parable about the persistent widow and the unjust judge to illustrate that "they should always pray and not give up" (v. 1). The verses above written by the prophet Isaiah eloquently reveal that God's praying people who give themselves and the Lord "no rest" will bring about the fulfillment of God's promises to His people. This is an awesome responsibility for us, and we need to take it seriously.

Too many Christians are under the impression that praying about the same thing again and again displeases God. Yet Jesus clearly instructed us about the importance of persistent prayer. I'm inclined to agree with those people who believe that it may be more offensive to God if we do *not* persist in prayer in certain matters. I've heard it said that many times believers lose heart and

LIVE ON PURPOSE TODAY

What have you been consistently praying for lately? Set your mind today to not quit praying in this area. When you feel like giving up, push harder. God will come through just in time.

give up praying just before their answer comes. The longer I walk with God, the more convinced I am that this is often the case. Since I have studied these verses and prayed for God's revelation, I have proven time and again that persistent prayer is fruitful and pleasing to God. But don't take my word for it. Try it yourself and discover firsthand how a loving God responds to our persistent pleas.

PRAYER

Lord, I'm sorry for the times I lost heart and gave up praying before You answered my prayer. I humbly ask You, as Your disciples did, "Lord, teach me to pray." Bless me with godly wisdom and help me to pray the prayers of Your heart. Give me the strength, courage, and faith I need to pray until the answer comes when it's Your will. Thank You for the harvest of answered prayer I'll reap as a result!

You Will Know Them by Their Fruit

When you follow the desires of your sinful nature, your lives will produce these evil results: sexual immorality, impure thoughts, eagerness for lustful pleasure, idolatry, participation in demonic activities, hostility, quarreling, jealousy, outbursts of anger, selfish ambition, divisions, the feeling that everyone is wrong except those in your own little group, envy, drunkenness, wild parties, and other kinds of sin. Let me tell you again, as I have before, that anyone living that sort of life will not inherit the Kingdom of God. But when the Holy Spirit controls our lives, He will produce this kind of fruit in us: love, joy, peace, patience, kindness, goodness, faithfulness, gentleness, and self-control.

GALATIANS 5:19-23 NLT

I recently heard from a young woman who was bitterly disappointed in a young man she had allowed herself to get close to. She was well acquainted with God's commands in Scripture that tell us, "Do not be yoked together with unbelievers..... What does a believer have in common with an unbeliever? 'Therefore, come out from them and be separate, says the Lord.'" (2 Cor. 6:14,15,17). And she was careful to make sure that her closest companions were Christians. But because she was so focused on this man's profession of faith, she failed to give serious attention to his un-Christlike behavior, and the relationship left her deeply hurt and disappointed.

As I prayed for this young woman and thought about her situation, the Lord impressed upon me a simple truth: A believer who *acts* like an unbeliever can do us just as much harm as someone who actually *is* an unbeliever. That's why the Scriptures command us to avoid close relationships with carnal (worldly) Christians. The apostle Paul wrote, "You are not to associate with anyone who claims to be a Christian yet indulges in sexual sin, or is greedy, or worships idols, or is abusive, or a drunkard, or a swindler. Don't even eat with such people" (1 Cor. 5:11 NLT). These sound like harsh guidelines for God's people, but they are necessary to prevent us from having a false sense of security around other Christians. I've seen many believers let their guard down around people they should have been more wary about, simply because these folks professed to be followers of Christ. Sadly, this casual attitude left these believers wide open to deception and destruction. Jesus said, "I am sending you out as sheep among wolves. Be as wary as snakes and harmless as doves" (Matt. 10:16 NLT). The Lord wants us to find the perfect balance between having suspicious minds and being gullible. He expects us to use godly discernment in all of our dealings with others. We can do that by being sensitive to the leading of the Holy Spirit and by having a working knowledge of God's Word.

LIVE ON PURPOSE TODAY

Read Galatians 5:22-23 in your Bible. Are you being the kind of person that you would want to be in a relationship with? If not, begin to ask the Holy Spirit to develop these fruits in your life.

Jesus said, "By their fruit you will recognize them" (Matt. 7:16). The Savior knew that others would try to deceive us, and that's why He warned us to put people to the test by examining their actions. He told us not to just pay attention to their words, but to look at how they live. He said, "Beware of false prophets who come disguised as harmless sheep, but are really wolves that will tear you apart. You can detect them by the way they act, just as you can identify a tree by its fruit" (Matt. 7:15,16 NLT). Though the Lord was referring to false prophets here, the principle is the same for others who would attempt to mislead God's people. Jesus goes on to say, "Not all people who sound religious are really godly. They may refer to Me as 'Lord,' but they still won't enter the Kingdom of Heaven. The decisive issue is whether they obey My Father in heaven" (Matt. 7:21 NLT). If the young woman who wrote me had given more attention to this man's actions and less to his words, she might have avoided being misled. But either because of ignorance or willfulness, she ignored the warning signs.

When we're faced with the possibility of forming a new relationship with someone, we shouldn't just ask ourselves, "Are they a Christian?" But the real question should be, "Would this relationship please and glorify God, and is it His will for me?" Scripture says, "Above all else, guard your affections. For they influence everything else in your life" (Prov. 4:23 TLB). The kind of relationships we make and maintain will affect every aspect of our lives, either positively or negatively. The choice is ours, and we should choose wisely.

PRAYER

Lord, teach me how to devote myself to prayer and the study of Your Word so that I may develop the spiritual discernment I need to avoid the relationships that are out of Your will for me. When I'm inclined to get close to someone, remind me to examine their "fruit" and to look for the characteristics that Your Word says believers should exhibit: "love, joy, peace, patience, kindness, goodness, faithfulness, gentleness, and self-control" (Gal. 5:22,23). Thank You that as I seek to please and glorify You with my relationships, You will bless me with godly, faithful, and loving companions!

The Truth About Sin

> *I have been crucified with Christ and I no longer live, but Christ lives in me. The life I live in the body I live by faith in the Son of God, who loved me and gave himself for me.*
>
> GALATIANS 2:20

Have you ever wondered why there are so many Christians today who are living lives of mediocrity instead of victory? Most likely it's because they haven't gotten a revelation of the truth of the above verses. If you have received salvation through Christ, you have been justified in the sight of God, and like the Scripture says, "If anyone is in Christ, he is a new creation; the old has gone, the new has come!" (2 Cor. 5:17). At the moment of salvation, you were changed on the inside. You were crucified with Christ, you died to the world, and you were "redeemed with the precious blood of Christ from worthless ways of living" (1 Peter 1:18). Colossians 3:3 AMP reads, "For [as far as this world is concerned] you have died, and your [new, real] life is hidden with Christ in God." Not only that, but the above verses confirm that at the time of your conversion, Christ Himself came to live on the inside of you through the Holy Spirit. But Satan wants you to believe that you're no different now than before you were saved. If he can convince you that you haven't changed on the inside, you will live a lifestyle that's not much different than a non-Christian's.

But once you get a revelation of your true identity in Christ and you walk in the light of the truth, you will no longer be a defeated Christian, but a victorious one. Once that happens you are on your way to sanctification, which is a process of growing spiritually and changing on the outside. How do we live sanctified lives in a fallen world? "By faith in the Son of God," as the verses above tell us. If you want your behavior to change so that it will be more like Christ's, then you will have to acknowledge your new identity in Christ, and you will have to resist Satan's attempts to deceive you. Of course there will be times when you sin, but the more you realize who you are in Christ, the more mature you will become spiritually and the less vulnerable you

LIVE ON PURPOSE TODAY

Do a search for Scriptures that contain the words "in Christ." Write as many of these Scriptures down as you can. Each one of these Scriptures represents a part of your identity in Christ. Meditate on the meaning of each Scripture and you will begin to see yourself as God sees you.

will be to temptation. First John 5:18 says, "We know that anyone born of God does not continue to sin; the one who was born of God keeps him safe, and the evil one cannot harm him." At the moment of salvation God equipped you with everything you need to live a godly life in an ungodly world. Now all you have to do is believe it. Jesus said that when we know the truth, the truth will set us free. (John 8:32.) It's my prayer that today you will begin to walk in the freedom that Christ gave His life to give you.

PRAYER

Lord, Your Word says that I should "consider myself dead to sin, but alive to God in Christ Jesus" (Rom. 6:11). Help me to do that, Lord. Cause me to realize who I really am in Christ. Show me how to walk in the light of Your truth so that the enemy cannot defeat me. I want my behavior to reflect Yours, Jesus. Thank You for setting me free so that I am free indeed! (John 8:32.)

Wait for the Harvest

Be patient, then, brothers, until the Lord's coming. See how the farmer waits for the land to yield its valuable crop and how patient he is for the autumn and spring rains. You, too, be patient and stand firm, because the Lord's coming is near.

JAMES 5:7,8

When my family became acquainted with Christian music years ago, we naturally wanted to share our enthusiasm with our friends and relatives. My boys, Joseph and John—who were teenagers at the time—seemed determined to get their teen cousins "turned on" to their new music. Whenever a gift-giving occasion came around, my boys would eagerly select and purchase music for their cousins that they had hoped would be a blessing to them. This went on for a few years, until finally my sister had to tactfully let me know that buying Christian music for her daughters was a waste. My boys were heartbroken, but we talked about the situation and decided to leave the matter in God's hands. I sympathized with my sons because I, too, had a desire to see my own sister take an interest in music that glorified the Lord. My attempts to introduce her to my music were unsuccessful, so I eventually gave up trying, and I began praying for God to change her heart. A year or two later one of the ladies my sister worked with began sharing her love for Christian music with my sis, who began developing a love of her own for it. Now my sister delights in introducing *me* to new music that glorifies God, and we have a new common bond between us that has made our relationship even stronger.

This experience was a reminder to me that when we plant seeds of faith in the hearts of others, we usually have to endure a waiting period. If you're like me, you not only want to impact others' lives for God, but you want to see the fruit of your labor right away. But the Lord used the verses above to remind me that, like farmers planting their crops need to be patient and wait for their valuable harvest, we must patiently wait to see the results of our efforts for God's kingdom. While these verses actually relate to the Lord's Second Coming, I also see a principle at work here that helps me to understand how we must often wait upon God to reveal His presence and power in people's lives and circumstances. Through our prayers, words, and actions, we can plant seeds in the lives of others that will produce a harvest for their good and God's glory. But if we become too frustrated or anxious, we could literally dig up the seeds we've planted before they've had a chance to take root and bear fruit. There have been many times when I've become impatient with the spiritual progress of those around me—especially my closest loved ones— and out of anger and frustration I've uprooted the seeds of faith I had tenderly planted in their hearts. In many cases it took months—or even years—to undo the damage I had done in just a short time. I've had to learn the hard way that planting a harvest for God takes time, patience, and understanding. Now when I begin to get anxious and impatient with the spiritual

LIVE ON PURPOSE TODAY

Do you believe you have reaped a harvest on all of the seed you have sown? If not, begin to pray over your seed. Believe that your harvest will come, whether in a few weeks or a few years, your harvest *will* come.

growth of others around me, I often think of my experience with my sister. It reminds me that even when it seems that my efforts are failing miserably, God could very well be working behind the scenes to make them fruitful somewhere down the line. I believe that as long as I am praying in faith and planting seeds according to God's leading, the Lord will keep working in that person's life somehow. I've seen God go to great lengths to put pressure on people and to surround them with believers, simply because I began praying for them and asking the Lord to change them. Now I take great comfort in knowing that even if I can't impact someone personally, God knows who can, and He will send the right person across their path as I pray for them in faith. I'm sharing all this with you today to encourage you not to give up on your efforts to influence others for God. Satan will try to convince you that all your prayers and seed planting are a waste of time and energy, but don't you believe it. Instead, put your hope in God, who's urging you today—"Be patient and stand firm, because the Lord's coming is near"!

PRAYER

Lord, when I'm tempted to become impatient with seeing the fruits of my labor for You, please remind me that my impatience can do more harm than good. Show me how to plant seeds of faith in people's lives and to nurture them with prayer, godly behavior, and understanding. Thank You for the valuable harvests that will bless many and glorify You!

Favor With God and Man

Let love and faithfulness never leave you; bind them around your neck, write them on the tablet of your heart. Then you will win favor and a good name in the sight of God and man.

PROVERBS 3:4

For most of my life I had repeatedly heard the verses in the Bible that talked about how those who were devoted to the Lord would suffer persecution and criticism from others. I got the impression that I always had to choose between having God's favor or man's. Once I started delving into the Scriptures, I realized that many times I could enjoy both. The verse above promises us favor in the sight of God *and* man when we walk in God's ways. The apostle Paul records a similar statement in Romans 14:18, where he describes true kingdom behavior and says, "Anyone who serves Christ in this way is pleasing to God and approved by men." The truth is that if we just concentrate on pleasing God, *He* will give us favor with others when we need it most. We can even *ask* God to give us favor with others. When we do that, we're not being selfish or prideful, but scriptural. Nehemiah was a devoted servant of the Lord. He was called by God to rebuild the city walls of Jerusalem during the reign of King Artaxerxes. As cupbearer to the king, he asked the Lord to give him favor with the ruler so that he could complete his God-given assignment. "Give Your servant success today by granting him favor in the presence of this man" (Neh. 1:11). Here we learn an important Bible principle—that God will grant us favor with others when it will help us carry out His will and plan. We can also pray for favor when we take a stand for the Lord. In the first chapter of the Book of Daniel, the young prophet "resolved not to defile himself with the royal food and wine," and he needed the cooperation of the chief official in order to carry out his commitment. Daniel 1:9 says, "Now God had caused the official to show favor and sympathy to Daniel." When receiving favor will glorify God, we shouldn't hesitate to pray for it.

It's true that believers who are really committed to God will sometimes experience criticism and persecution. Jesus said we could count on it. He wanted us to know what we were getting into when we made the decision to follow Him. If we're making a difference for God, we can't expect Satan to just sit back and do nothing to try to hinder us. But the Bible teaches us that we can pray for God's favor, which can be a powerful weapon against the enemy's attacks. Psalm 89:17 NLT says, "Our power is based on Your favor." And Psalm 5:12 says, "Surely, O Lord, You bless the righteous; You surround them with Your favor as with a shield." We are God's children, His chosen, His elect. And He is committed to protecting and providing for His own. When we concentrate on pleasing God, we can depend on Him to change people's hearts for our benefit. Proverbs 16:7 says, "When a man's ways are pleasing to the Lord, He makes even his enemies live at peace with him." If God is willing and able to change the hearts of

LIVE ON PURPOSE TODAY

Start every morning this week with a declaration of favor over your life. When you wake up, say aloud, "I have the favor of God over my life. I have favor with both God and man. Everywhere I go and everything I touch is blessed!"

our enemies, surely we can expect Him to give us favor in the sight of our teachers, employers, neighbors, and others we come in contact with. But we mustn't assume that this favor is automatic. Often we will have to ask God for it, expecting Him to act on our behalf. Over the years, when my children have been treated unfairly at school by their teachers or fellow students, I have asked the Lord to give them favor, and He has always been faithful. I have also asked God to grant my family favor in the sight of our bosses and coworkers. And I have seen my family acquire jobs that we were not even qualified for, often with salaries well above what we expected. When you pray for favor, people will bless you and they won't even know why. But don't just take my word for it. Begin today to pray for favor, and discover for yourself that "the Lord bestows favor and honor" upon His people! (Ps. 84:11).

PRAYER

Lord, help me to always concentrate on pleasing You, and teach me how to pray for favor with others, especially when I need it most. Reveal to me how praying for favor can open doors that appear to be closed. Thank You that blessing me with favor will bring You glory!

Our "Unrewarded" Work

There is going to come a time of testing at the judgment day to see what kind of work each builder has done. Everyone's work will be put through the fire to see whether or not it keeps its value. If the work survives the fire, that builder will receive a reward. But if the work is burned up, the builder will suffer great loss. The builders themselves will be saved, but like someone escaping through a wall of flames.

1 CORINTHIANS 3:13-15 NLT

Have you ever had days when you questioned why you were so committed to living the Christian life, doing the Lord's work? I have. Sometimes you look around and all you can see are people living for themselves, instead of the Lord. Many times it looks like unbelievers are being blessed more than we are. But I think what's the most disheartening is seeing so many Christians living mediocre lives. I'm referring to believers who go to church on Sunday, and maybe even are active in the church, but live lives devoid of a real passion for God. Often these same people look at you like you're some sort of fanatic because you aren't satisfied having a superficial relationship with God. Sometimes it's enough to make you want to scream—or cry.

I love the above verses by the apostle Paul. They remind me that when we get to heaven, all the things we did here out of love for the Lord will finally be rewarded. On the other hand, those believers who served themselves or served God with wrong motives will find that their rewards will not follow them into heaven. They themselves will be saved, but they'll have nothing to show for their lives after they leave here. But those of us who gave of our time and ourselves, often with little or no earthly reward, will find an abundance of heavenly rewards waiting for us. Remember all those prayers you prayed

LIVE ON PURPOSE TODAY

Look for an opportunity today to anonymously bless someone. Seek out 2-3 chances to secretly serve God where you will receive no recognition. Reflect on the reward of serving God rather than man.

when no one knew except you and God? What about all those times you said "no" to yourself when everyone else was doing what they pleased? And how about all the time you spent serving others, without ever seeing a single penny for it? Think of all the things you've done—or not done—out of love for the Lord that earned you little or no recognition or reward here on earth. These are the things that God holds closest to His heart. They are the very things that will bring you the greatest rewards from Him when you reach your heavenly home. And now I encourage you to "always give yourselves fully to the work of the Lord, because you know that your labor in the Lord is not in vain"! (1 Cor. 15:58).

PRAYER

Lord, when I'm tempted to think that You don't see or appreciate my efforts to please You, remind me that nothing I do for You is in vain. More importantly, keep me focused on You and Your will and not whether I'll be rewarded. Don't ever let me be satisfied with making a shallow commitment to You. Thank You that my devotion and dedication will allow You to use me in awesome ways for Your glory!

Dealing With Doubt

*When the [evil] spirit saw Jesus, it immediately threw the boy
into a convulsion. He fell to the ground and rolled around,
foaming at the mouth. Jesus asked the boy's father,
"How long has he been like this?" "From childhood," he
answered. "It has often thrown him into fire or water to kill
him. But if you can do anything, take pity on us and help us."
"'If you can?'" said Jesus. "Everything
is possible for him who believes."
Immediately the boy's father exclaimed,
"I do believe; help me overcome my unbelief!"*

MARK 9:20-24

In the above passage, a man whose son is possessed by an evil
spirit appeals to Jesus to deliver the boy from his torment. We
discover in the preceding verses that the disciples had just
attempted to drive out the demon and failed. Who could blame
this father for his doubts? When he appeals to the Messiah for
help, Jesus indicates that the man's own faith plays a part in
whether or not his son will receive a miracle. It is then that this
parent pleads with the Savior to help him believe. How does Jesus
respond? He doesn't say, "Well, you've just missed your chance for
a miracle, and now your son will just have to learn to live with
that demon!" No, Jesus responds by casting the foul spirit out of
the boy forever.

Some Christians believe that in certain matters our faith has
to be perfect before we can receive anything from God. I used to

believe that myself. Some believe that we shouldn't ask God to increase our faith because it might displease Him, and He probably wouldn't do it anyway. Now I believe that in times of doubt, that father's exclamation is one of the best prayers I can pray. Ephesians 2:8-9 says that our faith is a gift from God. And Hebrews 12:2 says that Jesus is the "author and perfecter of our faith." The Bible makes it clear that our faith is a gift from God, perfected by God, so why do we berate ourselves when we can't muster up the faith we think we should have? I do believe Scripture reveals that doubt and unbelief are sins against God, and because of that we need to resist them like other sins. But if we are permitted, and even expected, to ask God for help to overcome other sins, why can't we do the same when we're struggling with doubt? In addition to prayer, there are other things we can do to cooperate with God's faith-building plan for us. The Bible says that God's Word builds our faith. (Rom. 10:17; Acts 20:32.) So, we can devote ourselves to studying, memorizing, and meditating on the Scriptures. And we

LIVE ON PURPOSE TODAY

What have you been listening to lately? Are you listening to conversations of unbelief, worldly television, or negative music? Make sure that you are listening to the Word of God as much as possible. Fill your empty time with the Word rather than the world's choices. Do this and your faith will increase.

can spend time listening to good preaching and teaching. But let us not forget that in times of doubt we can pray like the Savior's own disciples did—"Lord, increase our faith!" (Luke 17:5).

PRAYER

*Lord, I want so much to have perfect faith, but sometimes
I must confess that I struggle with doubt. During those times
I ask You to help me overcome my unbelief. Increase my faith
daily, and teach me to do my part so that I can cooperate with
You for the perfecting of my faith. Thank You for giving
me the faith I need to receive all that You have for me!*

Waiting for God's Best

Yet the Lord longs to be gracious to you;
he rises to show you compassion.
For the Lord is a God of justice.
Blessed are all who wait for him!

ISAIAH 30:18

No one likes to wait. Especially these days. Our society is used to having what we want, when we want it. But this is not God's way. The Bible is filled with stories and verses about the value of waiting on God. In God's kingdom, timing is everything. If you look at the lives of most of the great men and women of the Bible, you see that they had to endure long periods of waiting before their God-given purpose was fulfilled. Abraham had to wait many years before his promised son was born. Moses was 80 years old before God called him to lead the Israelites out of Egypt. Joseph endured long years of injustice before Pharoah put him in charge of all Egypt. David suffered many years of persecution at the hands of Saul before he became king. And the list goes on. God used periods of waiting to prepare these people for the extraordinary blessings He had in store for them.

Sometimes it seems that God has put us on a shelf. It can be bewildering, frustrating, and depressing. We have a hard time trying to imagine any good coming out of it. One of the hardest parts is having to face all of the well-meaning people who keep saying, "What are you going to do?" You feel like you've done all that you can do. But that doesn't stop you from trying to come up

LIVE ON PURPOSE TODAY

Have you been working on your own accord to try to "make something happen" in your life? Maybe it's a relationship or job issue. Whatever it is, slow down and wait patiently on God's timing. Begin today to move at God's perfect pace and receive all that He has planned for you.

with something. Then it occurs to you that maybe there's a way you can "help God." And you try to think of ways to "make something happen." Listen. If you really want to help God—trust Him. When He makes you wait, there's a good reason for it. The fact is, there are some blessings we are never going to receive unless we wait for them. Yes, these times of waiting are uncomfortable for us. Sometimes they're downright painful. But if we try to make our own way instead of waiting on God, we will miss out on God's best for us. Let me encourage you today with some words from a man who had to do a lot of waiting in his life, but who was blessed beyond belief. In Psalm 27:14, David says, "Wait for the Lord; be strong and take heart, and wait for the Lord"!

PRAYER

Lord, You know how hard waiting is for me. Please give me the patience I need to wait for Your perfect timing in everything. Help me not to settle for second best. When I'm tempted to "make something happen," speak to my heart and remind me what my impatience can cost me. Help me to not only wait, but to do so with a good attitude. Thank You for all the blessings You have in store for me!

Pouring Out Our Complaints

I cry out to the Lord; I plead for the Lord's mercy. I pour out my complaints before him and tell him all my troubles.

PSALM 142:1,2 NLT

There was a time when I thought that voicing my complaints to the Lord was offensive to Him. But when I began studying the Scriptures seriously, I realized that many of the people in the Bible whom God honored the most often poured their complaints out to Him. I love the depth of emotion revealed in the Book of Psalms. Those psalmists are real people I can really relate to. They express their anger, indignation, fear, joy, and almost every other emotion with honesty and sincerity. In Psalm 145:18, David writes, "The Lord is near to all who call on him, to all who call on him in truth." We have a God who wants to have an intimate relationship with His people. For that intimacy to be genuine, we have to be able to speak to God truthfully. He knows what we're feeling inside. We can't hide anything from Him. So why do we try to cover up our negative feelings as though if we don't acknowledge them, they'll just go away?

The Bible says that God called David "a man after my own heart" (Acts 13:22). It was David who penned the verses above in Psalm 142. The Scriptures reveal that he often poured his complaints out to God. Yet God loved him and honored him in awesome ways. God knew that David's heart was right toward Him. David didn't go around grumbling and complaining about how God was treating him. David took his complaints straight to God. And that's what we need to do, too. If we don't go to the Lord with our grievances, we'll end up going to other people. If we do that, we can end up taking unwise advice or grieving others' hearts, especially when they feel helpless to aid us. We need to go to the only One who is equipped to solve our problems and meet our deepest needs. I'm not saying that it's always wrong to share our troubles with other people. I'm saying that at least most of the time we should take our complaints directly to God. This is especially true if we are complaining about other people. God might well understand our coming to Him with grievances about other people, but if we voice them to others He might consider it gossip, in which case He will not be pleased. Also, the more we talk about others to other people, the more angry and indignant we often become. But if we have that same conversation with God, we will feel a sense of relief afterwards. We can ask the Lord to forgive us for our grievances and to cleanse us of all anger and resentment. And if we're being treated unfairly, we can ask God to work justice for us. In Psalm 62:8, David says, "Pour out your heart to him." My prayer is that you will take David's advice and open the door to a new level of intimacy with the Lord. Be encouraged today with this precious verse from

LIVE ON PURPOSE TODAY

Complaining can destroy your life. Ask a person you trust to hold you accountable for your words. Ask the Holy Spirit to also help you restrain your complaints by bringing them to your attention *before* you speak. Finally, feed on the Word and you will find fewer things to complain about.

the psalmist's pen: "I took my troubles to the Lord; I cried out to him, and he answered my prayer"! (Ps. 120:1 NLT).

PRAYER

Lord, teach me to pour out my complaints to You, instead of to others. Remind me that You are the only One who can really help me when I'm in need. Give me an understanding of how much You love me and desire to be my everything. Show me how to have a genuine and intimate relationship with You. Thank You that I never need to feel guilty or condemned for sharing my true feelings with You!

My Father Is Greater Than All

My Father, who has given them to Me, is greater than all.

JOHN 10:29

Recently, when I was going through a very difficult time and earnestly seeking the Lord, He brought it to my attention that I was focusing entirely too much on the devil and not enough on God. As a result, I was feeling more and more fearful, depressed, and hopeless. The Lord led me to the Scripture above, and He impressed upon me to meditate on the phrase, "My Father is greater than all." Every time negative feelings threatened to overwhelm me, I reminded myself of this powerful truth, and I could sense a calmness crowding out my fears.

I often hear from people who say something like, "The devil is really doing a number on me!" I can really sympathize with them because I know those feelings all too well myself. The good news is that if we will make the effort to remind ourselves of some powerful truths from God's Word, we can be the overcomers that the Lord wants us to be. First of all, we need to remember that only God is all-powerful. Also, God limits the activities of Satan and his demonic forces. And to some extent, we can, too. James 4:7 says, "Submit yourselves to God. Resist the devil, and he will flee from you." By sinning, we can give Satan the opportunity to come into our lives to "steal, kill and destroy" (John 10:10). But by living in submission to God's will and resisting temptation when it comes, we can slam the door in the devil's face and severely limit his involvement in our lives.

Another way we can hinder Satan's activities against us is to "pray without ceasing," like the Bible says (1 Thess. 5:17 KJV). For those of us who belong to the Lord, prayer should be like breathing. We are in a continuous battle with the forces of evil, and by keeping in constant communication with our divine Commander-in-Chief and relying on His power and guidance, we can avoid a lot of the traps and obstacles that the enemy puts in our way. As we give God first place in our lives, and as we trust and obey Him in every situation, we can count on Him to fight our battles for us so that we can live the life of rest and peace that He's called us to. (Heb. 4:3; Col. 3:15.)

If you have put your hope in Christ, then you have been equipped with heavenly weapons to be an overcomer. I urge you to make a commitment to dig into God's Word and discover for yourself how the Lord has provided you with everything you need to walk in victory. The apostle John reminds us that because we have been born of God, the One who lives in us (God) is greater than the one who is in the world (Satan). (1 John 4:4.) And Paul reminds us that the Lord is not neutral when he writes, "If God is for us, who can be against us?" (Rom. 8:31). On

LIVE ON PURPOSE TODAY

Write down all the trials you are facing today on a sheet of paper. Beside each one, write out a Scripture to stand on for that particular situation. Keep that piece of paper where you can see it every day and focus on what God's Word promises instead of the trial.

our own we can do nothing. (John 15:5.) But with God on our side, "we are more than conquerors" (Rom. 8:37).

It's true that Satan is a formidable opponent. But he's no match for God. When we fear the devil and concentrate on his activities, we actually play into his hands and give him the kind of attention and control he thrives on. But when we keep our eyes on God and attend to His Word, we strengthen our defenses against satanic attack. The next time you are in a trial and are feeling "under attack," make a conscious decision to focus not on the devil's destructiveness, but on God's greatness. Take heart and remember the Savior's words—your Father is greater than all!

PRAYER

Lord, help me to focus on Your greatness and goodness when I'm going through difficult times. When I'm tempted to fear the devil and his activities, remind me that as long as I fear and reverence You alone, I need fear nothing else. (Isa. 8:13,14.) Teach me how to encourage myself with the truth of Your Word so that I'll have a keen awareness of who I am in Christ and who You are to me. Thank You for fighting my battles and enabling me to live a life of victory and rest!

Expecting God To Act

> *But when you ask him, be sure that you really expect him to answer, for a doubtful mind is as unsettled as a wave of the sea that is driven and tossed by the wind. People like that should not expect to receive anything from the Lord.*
>
> JAMES 1:6,7 NLT

In these verses, James reveals an essential ingredient for answered prayer. Though he is referring to a request for divine wisdom here, the basic principle he reveals in this passage can be applied to almost any petition we make to the Lord. The key word here is "expect." James says that if we pray, but don't really expect God to answer us, we shouldn't be surprised if He doesn't. The dictionary defines *expect* as: "To anticipate in the mind,"[2] and the thesaurus lists *await, count, hope,* and *look* as synonyms for *expect.*[3] These are many of the terms that the authors of the Bible use, especially in the Psalms. I thought it was interesting that the thesaurus listed "despair of" as the opposite of *expect.* I've often felt that the antidote for fear and despair was expecting God to act on our behalf, and here I saw it confirmed in a dictionary. Many psalms begin with the psalmist crying out to God in desperation and despair. But often by the end of the psalm, the author is praising and thanking the Lord in advance for all that He will do for him. What happened in those interim verses? The psalmist chose to expect God to act on his behalf. By an act of his will, he made a decision to take his stand in bold expectation. A good example of this is in Psalm 42. Verses 9-10 TLB say, "'O God my Rock,' I cry, 'why have you forsaken me? Why must I suffer these attacks from my enemies?' Their taunts pierce me like a fatal wound; again and again they scoff, 'Where is that God of yours?'" But the next, and final, verse says, "But O my soul, don't be discouraged. Don't be upset. Expect God to act! For I know that I shall again have plenty of reason to praise him for all that he will do. He is my help! He is my God!"

Jesus said, "Whatever you ask for in prayer, believe that you have received it, and it will be yours" (Mark 11:24). The Master is telling us here that if we want God to answer our prayers, we must expect an answer from Him. We know that God called David a man after His own heart. David's verses throughout the Bible are filled with expectation. He writes, "In the morning I lay my requests before you and wait in expectation" (Ps. 5:3). And in Psalm 27:14 AMP, David urges us, "Wait and hope for and expect the Lord." Expecting God to act on our behalf shows the Lord that we truly believe in Him and His Word. Psalm 130:5 TLB says, "I wait expectantly, trusting God to help, for He has promised." I can't guarantee that if you expect an answer each time you pray, you'll always get what you asked for. But I can tell you this—if you pray with a lively expectation, your percentage of answered prayer will increase dramatically. I have seen it in my own life, as well as in the lives of others. And having

LIVE ON PURPOSE

Are you expecting anything from God today? Make a list of all the things you are exercising your faith for from God. Every few weeks, read over the list and begin to mark the items that God completes. This list will eventually become your list of testimonies!

an attitude of expectancy will produce a peace and joy in our hearts that we would not have otherwise. If you're waiting on God right now for something, wait expectantly, for "the Lord is good to those who hopefully and expectantly wait for Him" (Lam. 3:25 AMP). May this declaration of faith by the psalmist be ours today and always: "I will keep expecting you to help me. I praise you more and more"! (Ps. 71:14 TLB).

PRAYER

Lord, teach me how to pray with an attitude of expectancy. Guard me from the fear and doubt that would hinder me from receiving an answer. In times of waiting, give me a lively expectation that will sustain me with Your peace and joy. Thank You that my bountiful harvest of answered prayer will bless many and glorify You!

Commit to Victory

Commit your way to the Lord, trust also in Him,
and He shall bring it to pass.

PSALM 37:5 NKJV

I'm a member of the "Baby Boomers" generation. We've been called the "Me" generation, and with good reason. We were taught to be self-sufficient and independent, and to "look out for number one." We were told to concentrate on meeting our own needs because no one else would. There's just one problem with this mentality. It doesn't work. This is evident in the fact that more people are on tranquilizers and antidepressants today than ever before. More are resorting to alcohol and drug abuse. More marriages are ending in divorce. More families are falling apart. And more people are going from one destructive relationship to another. As long as we are looking to the world for solutions, we will get the same results they're getting—defeat, despair, and emptiness. But believers don't have to live that way. Jesus said that He came that we might live the abundant life. (John 10:10.) But living His way is a choice we must make; He won't force it on us. The reason we don't see more believers living "the higher life" that God offers is because many are unwilling to submit to His will. Because of pride or rebellion they've chosen to do things their own way, instead of God's. Often they're afraid of what living for the Lord will cost them. They haven't gotten the revelation yet that God cares about their happiness and well-being even more than they do. They aren't convinced that God created them with a specific purpose in mind, and that only by fulfilling this purpose will they find the peace, joy, and contentment they so desperately want and need.

God wants to solve our problems and meet our needs, but He requires our cooperation. That's why the verse above instructs us to commit our ways to the Lord and trust in Him to act on our behalf. When we do this, we are essentially telling Him, "Lord, I surrender all that I am and all that I have to You. Work Your perfect will in my life, and use me for Your glory." In Isaiah 55:9, God says, "As the heavens are higher than the earth, so are My ways higher than your ways and My thoughts than your thoughts." We will never know God in an intimate way through reasoning. He's so far above our level of understanding that we can only come to know Him and His ways by revelation. That's why we need faith. We've got to believe that God loves us and wants the best for us, and that He's infinitely wiser than we are. Isaiah 48:17 says, "I am the Lord your God, who teaches you what is best for you, who directs you in the way you should go." When we commit our lives to God each day, He will not only direct us, but He will re-direct us, if necessary. But if we have our own plans "engraved in stone," we don't leave any room for God to lead us or to change our direction. Human

LIVE ON PURPOSE TODAY

Ask God to reveal any area where your actions have displeased Him. Ask His forgiveness and seek His direction in that area. Make a decision to change today. Write your decision down in your Bible so that you have a reminder of when you decided to do it God's way. Later, refer back and see how God has changed your life.

nature being what it is, even just hearing the word *submission* can make us cringe. But if our minds are renewed to God's truth, we can remind ourselves that submitting to God opens the door to the supernatural. Anytime we agree to do things God's way, we tap into an inexhaustible source of possibilities. When that happens, even the surest defeat can be transformed into the greatest victory. Another thing to consider is the fact that when we wholeheartedly commit ourselves to the Lord, He becomes responsible for our protection and provision. So being in God's will is always the safest place to be. On the other hand, being out of God's will makes us more vulnerable to Satan's attacks. First John 2:17 AMP says, "The world passes away and disappears, and with it the forbidden cravings (the passionate desires, the lust) of it; but he who does the will of God and carries out His purposes in his life abides (remains) forever." It's true that if you choose God's plans and purposes for your life, you'll lose much of what this world has to offer. But rest assured that the rewards you gain will last an eternity!

PRAYER

*Lord, I commit myself, my family, my finances, my work,
my ministry—all that I am and all that I have—to You today.
Work Your perfect will in them and use them for Your glory.
I commit all my needs to You, Lord—all my healing, financial,
material, social, emotional, and ministry needs. Supply them
abundantly, according to Your promise. (Phil. 4:19.) Thank You,
Lord, that You are "More Than Enough" ("El Shaddai")!*

Noble Vessels

> *In a large house there are articles not only of gold and silver,*
> *but also of wood and clay; some are for noble purposes and*
> *some for ignoble. If a man cleanses himself from the latter,*
> *he will be an instrument for noble purposes, made holy,*
> *useful to the Master and prepared to do any good work.*
>
> 2 TIMOTHY 2:20,21

In these verses, the apostle Paul is urging us to become the kind of believers that God can use for His highest purposes. Paul says that those most useful to the Lord are those who "cleanse" themselves from things that do not honor God. I've noticed a pattern developing in my own life that has illustrated this principle clearly. It seems that whenever the Lord has brought me up to a higher level of service, it has often been after I've "cleansed" myself of a questionable practice, behavior, or association. For example, I had read the books of a certain novelist for many years, and I enjoyed them immensely. But the last time I bought one and began reading it, I felt convicted. I prayed about it but got no clear direction from the Lord. Then I made what was a very tough decision for me. I threw the book in the garbage. I'd like to say that I felt good afterwards, but the truth is that I felt awful. Some weeks later the Lord opened a wonderful door of opportunity for me, and when He did, He let me know that it was partly because I threw that book away. He knew what a sacrifice it was for me, and He honored me for it.

So what are some of the things that God might call us to "cleanse" ourselves from? Various forms of entertainment and relationships are just two areas that may be involved. Think about the TV, movies, books, magazines, video games, and music that you expose yourself to. Ask yourself—does it honor God or dishonor Him? Be honest with yourself and with God. For instance, is there any music you listen to that might be considered "objectionable"? Does it lift you up or bring you down? Does it make you feel closer to God or further away from Him? I listened to secular music for decades, and I enjoyed it very much. Eventually, I made the decision to listen only to Christian music. You think it's hard to give up secular music if you're a teenager? Try doing it after you've listened to it for decades, as I have. Was it tough? Yes. Was it worth it? Yes! Jesus said, "No one who puts his hand to the plow and looks back is fit for service in the kingdom of God" (Luke 9:62). When I'm tempted to look back longingly at some of the things I've given up, I resist that urge because I know that God is not

LIVE ON PURPOSE TODAY

Each one of us has an area that God desires to cleanse us from. Spend some time today in prayer asking God to reveal this area to you. If you want to go deeper in your relationship with God, then act on His directives. Remove any barriers in your life to being cleansed by God. This is the first step to spiritual maturity.

pleased with that kind of attitude. The Lord has even led me to discontinue some longtime friendships that were hindering my walk with Him. And every time I obeyed, God made the separation far easier than I ever anticipated. Don't settle for less than

God's best in your life, but be prepared to do whatever it takes to become a "noble vessel" who is "useful to the Master." Discover for yourself that God means it when He says, "Those who honor Me, I will honor" (1 Sam. 2:30).

PRAYER

Lord, don't let me miss out on Your highest purposes for my life. Give me the desire and the grace I need to cleanse myself of all that would hinder me from receiving Your best. Let Your Spirit convict me when I'm out of Your will, and help me to respond promptly in obedience. Thank You for the honors I'll receive as a result!

Look for What God Can Do

Jesus said, "You're asking the wrong question. You're looking
for someone to blame. There is no such cause-effect here.
Look instead for what God can do."

JOHN 9:3 MESSAGE

T he Lord showed me this verse from The Message Bible
when I was seeking Him about the serious problems my
husband and I were having with our oldest son. I was
asking God questions like: "What went wrong? Where did I fail?
What could I have done differently?" And I was driving myself
crazy. The only answer I ever really got from the Lord was the
above verse. He obviously didn't want me trying to assign blame
to someone or something. He wanted me to put aside my questions and regrets and to focus instead on what He was willing and
able to do in the matter. And I got the distinct impression that He
wasn't going to do *anything* until I took my eyes off my problems
and put them on Him.

Whenever we're experiencing trials, it's a good idea to ask
the Lord how we might have caused or contributed to them in any
way. If we do this with a sincere and open heart, we can depend
on Him to reveal our wrongdoing. Then we can confess it, receive
His forgiveness, and ask for His help not to repeat the offense. But
sometimes He doesn't show us anything in particular that we have
done wrong. When that's the case, we can either start dredging up
all kinds of imagined offenses and focus on all the things that are
wrong with us—or we can enter God's rest, keeping our eyes on

Him and trusting in His willingness and ability to bring good out of the situation. Unfortunately, the last thing Satan wants is for us to rest in the Lord. More than likely, he'll bring people along our path who will begin to suggest that we *must* have done something wrong or we wouldn't be having

LIVE ON PURPOSE TODAY

What are you "digging" on that God wants you to leave behind? Ask Him for His help and leave those questions in the past. Begin to enter into His rest and put down your shovel today.

these problems. Then we can start feeling guilty and condemned, which is exactly what the devil wanted in the first place. When there's no doubt that our own foolishness is somehow responsible for our problems, we can expect Satan to say something to us like: "You don't *really* expect God to help you out of this mess. After all, you brought it on by your *own* stupidity!" Even if that's true, it would be even more foolish not to seek or accept help from the only One who can really rescue us. While it's true that our God is a righteous Judge, it's also true that He is exceedingly merciful, especially toward those who love and reverence Him. Psalm 103:10-11 says, "He does not treat us as our sins deserve or repay us according to our iniquities. For as high as the heavens are above the earth, so great is His love for those who fear Him." And verses 14-15 NKJV assure us, "As a father pities His children, so the Lord pities those who fear Him. For He knows our frame; He remembers that we are dust." The Lord *did* reveal His glory in my situation with my son, and I believe that shifting my focus from the problem to the Problem Solver made all the difference. If you are in a hard place today, know that God doesn't want you spending all your time and energy trying to figure out why. That won't please or glorify Him. Instead, put your questions and regrets aside and start looking for what God can do!

PRAYER

Lord, when I'm experiencing trials, help me to seek You about anything I might have done to contribute to them. When I'm tempted to go on a "digging expedition"—trying to come up with all kinds of things I might have done to cause my troubles— remind me that this is not Your will for me. Help me instead to enter Your rest by focusing on You and Your promises. Thank You that as I keep my eyes on You, I will be blessed and You will be glorified!

The Importance of Joy

The joy of the Lord is your strength.

NEHEMIAH 8:10

In the Bible, the concept of joy is serious business. It's not a superficial warm and fuzzy kind of feeling. It's a fruit of the Spirit (Gal. 5:22), and it can help the believer overcome all kinds of adversity. The verse above reveals that we gain strength from the joy that God gives us. And the Scriptures indicate that when we lose our joy, we can become victims of despair and even sickness. Proverbs 17:22 TLB says, "A cheerful heart does good like a medicine, but a broken spirit makes one sick." Have you ever gotten sick after something happened to disappoint or depress you? I have. Next time you're ill, ask yourself if you've been struggling with negative emotions. Proverbs 15:15 TLB says, "When a man is gloomy, everything seems to go wrong; when he is cheerful, everything seems right!" Ever notice how your moods can affect your whole outlook on life? When you're feeling down, it can seem like nothing's going right and everyone around you irritates you. But if you're feeling particularly cheerful one day, almost nothing bothers you. When you're filled with the joy of the Lord, you feel strong, capable, and ready for anything. That's why a joy-filled believer is hard for the devil to handle. If the enemy can steal your joy, he can rob you of almost anything, including your health.

Romans 14:17 says that the kingdom of God is "righteousness, peace, and joy in the Holy Spirit." That should tell us just

LIVE ON PURPOSE TODAY

Joy is a powerful force. Ask God to send you His supernatural joy throughout the day today, and feel yourself grow strong in His life-changing joy.

how valuable joy is to the believer. Jesus spoke about joy a lot. It was the Savior's desire that His disciples would be filled with joy. (John 16:22; 17:13.) In John 16:24, Jesus says, "Ask, using my name, and you will receive, and you will have abundant joy." And in 1 Thessalonians 5:6, Paul writes, "Be joyful always." The Bible tells us that God wants us to serve Him with joy. Psalm 100:2 says, "Serve the Lord with gladness." And Deuteronomy 28:47 says that because God's people refused to serve Him joyfully, He would cause them to serve their enemies instead. The Lord deserves to have us serve Him with joy, and He's given us His Holy Spirit as our source of joy. Let me encourage you to memorize Psalm 86:4 so that the next time you need a fresh dose of joy, you can pray like David did, "Bring joy to your servant, for to you, O Lord, I lift up my soul." Before you know it, you'll be filled with the joy of the Lord, and nothing will be able to keep you down!

PRAYER

Lord, I ask that by Your Spirit You would fill me with everlasting joy. Give me a happy heart and a cheerful mind so that I may walk in wholeness. Whenever I'm tempted to despair, remind me of the importance of joy and how You deserve a cheerful servant. Thank You that Your joy makes me strong!

God's Perfect Plan for Us

"For I know the plans I have for you,"
declares the Lord, "plans to prosper you and not
to harm you, plans to give you hope and a future."

JEREMIAH 29:11

I recently had an interesting discussion with a family member who said that he wasn't convinced that God had a perfect plan for every believer. I begged to differ with him. The promise above belongs to every child of God, and it's important that all of us believe it and live each day of our lives as though it's true. If we don't, we are at risk of spending a lifetime trying to figure out where we should go, what we should do, and who we should be with. God told the prophet Jeremiah, "Before I formed you in the womb I knew you, before you were born I set you apart; I appointed you as a prophet to the nations" (Jer. 1:5). Our call may be different from Jeremiah's, but it's just as important for us to fulfill our purpose as it was for Jeremiah to fulfill his. We are not called to duplicate or imitate anyone else in this life. We are called to become all that God has destined us to be. When we hand God the "steering wheel" of our lives—giving Him complete control— He begins to unveil His plans for us one step at a time. He usually doesn't reveal the "big picture" to us all at once, because we'd either become fearful or have an attitude that says, "Okay, God—I can take it from here!" The Lord knows that we need His constant help, so He wisely encourages our dependence on Him.

So why are so many believers afraid of surrendering them-selves to God? Perhaps they are afraid that the Lord would ask them to do something they despise, or something that doesn't fit their idea of success. The truth is that we can never be truly happy or successful apart from fulfilling our God-given purpose. Suppose the Lord created you to be a bus driver. He could abundantly supply all your needs, and fill your life with real purpose and meaning as a bus driver, simply because that's your God-given call in life. But suppose you decide you don't want to be a bus driver—you'd rather be a teacher. So you go through all of the expense and training of becoming a teacher, and you never find true peace, joy, or satisfaction because you're living your life doing something that God never created you to do. There's always something missing in your life, and you can't deny the emptiness you feel every time you have to face a new day. The truth of the matter is that because God called you to be a bus driver, He has equipped you to enjoy being one. You surely

LIVE ON PURPOSE TODAY

Write down your dreams. Commit them to God. Ask Him to speak to you His vision and direction for your life.

won't enjoy every aspect of your call, but it doesn't matter so much because you have a deep-down satisfaction in your soul that says, "This feels right for me." Sadly, a lot of believers don't follow their God-given call simply because of what other people might say or think. Then they wonder why they aren't experiencing the abundant life that Jesus died to give them.

Ephesians 2:10 says, "For we are God's workmanship, created in Christ Jesus to do good works, which God prepared in advance for us to do." When God designed you, He equipped you with everything you would need to fulfill your God-given purpose. He's given you gifts and skills that He wants to help you develop over the course of your life. If you ask Him what they are, He'll show you. He may direct you to get some special education or training, or He may not. The key to fulfilling your God-given call is to seek the Lord *daily*. Don't wait until you're at a crossroads in your life, having to make an important decision that will affect your whole future. If you do, chances are that you will significantly delay receiving the rich rewards God has in store for you. Hebrews 11:6 says, "You can never please God without faith, without depending on him. Anyone who wants to come to God must believe that there is a God and that he rewards those who sincerely look for him." If you live your life depending on God's wisdom, guidance, and grace daily, you can count on Him to lead you in the path of His greatest blessings. The truth is that there is *no way* for us to improve on God's perfect plan for our lives. The sooner we get a hold of this truth, the sooner we can begin cooperating with Him to bring it to pass in our lives—and the sooner we can begin reaping His blessed rewards!

PRAYER

Lord, I believe that You created me for a special purpose and that You have a perfect plan for my life. I ask that You fulfill Your purpose for me, and help me to do my part by earnestly seeking You daily through prayer and Your Word. Thank You that as I seek You each day, You will "guide me along the best pathway for my life"! (Ps. 32:8 NLT).

Friendships According to God

The righteous should choose his friends carefully,
for the way of the wicked leads them astray.

PROVERBS 12:26 NKJV

The above verse reveals that God expects us to use godly wisdom and discernment in making friends. Jesus had thousands of followers and hundreds of disciples, but He chose only twelve men to spend most of His time with. And His "inner circle" consisted of only three men—Peter, James, and John. If the Son of God was so careful about whom He chose as His close companions, shouldn't we be at least as careful? Amos 3:3 NKJV says, "Can two walk together unless they are agreed?" No, they can't. That means that if we are walking with unbelievers, we are going to have to make some compromises to stay in relationship with them. And those compromises will come between us and God. Proverbs 13:20 says, "He who walks with the wise grows wise, but a companion of fools suffers harm." We see evidence of this truth all around us—God's people who mistakenly believe that they can be in relationship with unbelievers without suffering the consequences. The apostle Paul wrote, "Do not be misled: 'Bad company corrupts good character'" (1 Cor. 15:33). We like to think we are immune to the negative influences of wrong companionships, but the Lord knows otherwise, and that's why He has so much to say about the subject in His Word. In 2 Corinthians 6, Paul writes, "Do not be yoked together with unbelievers.... What does a believer have in common with an unbeliever?.... 'Therefore, come out from them and be separate, says the Lord.'" (vv. 14,15,17). God makes it clear that it's absolutely essential for our closest companions to be people who love the Lord. If they aren't, how can they hold us accountable as Christians? Proverbs 27:6 NKJV says, "Faithful are the wounds of a friend, but the kisses of an enemy are deceitful." Our real friends will correct us when we need it, while a false friend will only tell us what we want to hear, even if we're doing wrong and are headed for destruction. For those who have a desire to be popular, God gives this warning in Proverbs 18:24 NASB: "A man of many friends comes to ruin." If you don't have a lot of friends, don't despair. God's Word indicates that you may be even more blessed having only one or two close friends than having more.

So, what kind of friends does God want us to have? The psalmist tells us in Psalm 119:63 NKJV, "I am a companion of all those who fear You, and of those who keep Your precepts." Our closest friends should love the Lord and seek to please Him. If your closest companions are not believers, you are out of God's will, and you need to seek the Lord and ask Him how to separate yourself from these associations. I know from experience that He will show you how. When I first began getting serious about my relationship with the Lord, I had some close friends who did not know God. Some of these friendships were decades old, and it

LIVE ON PURPOSE TODAY

Examine your relationships with your close friends. Are they a godly influence? If not, begin to distance yourself and ask God to help you sever your ties with them. Pray that God will send you good Christian friends.

grieved my heart to think of ending them. But after seeking God's wisdom and guidance, I put these relationships on the altar and asked Him to help me sever these ties in a way that would please and glorify Him. I won't say that it wasn't painful or difficult for me at times, but I must tell you that the Lord gave me a peace and reassurance that I still can't explain. If you don't have some close believing friends, then you need to earnestly ask God for some. But keep in mind that He may not answer your prayer until you step out in faith and begin distancing yourself from any unbelieving companions you have in your life right now. You may even have to endure a period of loneliness. If you do, you will have the opportunity to prove to God, yourself, and others that you are serious about pleasing Him in this area. And the Lord will reward you with new and exciting "divine connections" that will bless you and bring you closer to Him. If you are a child of the King, you don't ever have to feel lonely or abandoned. Jesus Himself said, "I will not abandon you as orphans—I will come to you" (John 14:18 NLT). And He wants to be your closest friend. (John 15:15.) Today, open up your heart and let the Savior be to you all that He longs to be, and experience for yourself true friendship at its best!

PRAYER

Lord, when I'm tempted to satisfy my emotional and social needs outside of Your will, please strengthen me and remind of how much it could cost me. Show me how to separate myself from my wrong associations, and give me godly companions who will encourage my devotion to You. Thank You that I need never feel alone or abandoned because You are always near! (Heb. 13:5.)

Step Out in Faith

*During the fourth watch of the night Jesus went out to them,
walking on the lake. When the disciples saw him walking
on the lake, they were terrified. "It's a ghost," they said,
and cried out in fear. But Jesus immediately said to them:
"Take courage! It is I. Don't be afraid."
"Lord, if it's you," Peter replied, "tell me to come to you
on the water."
"Come," he said. Then Peter got down out of the boat, walked on
the water and came toward Jesus. But when he saw the wind, he
was afraid and, beginning to sink, cried out, "Lord, save me!"
Immediately Jesus reached out his hand and caught him.
"You of little faith," he said, "why did you doubt?"*

MATTHEW 14:25-31

Peter was actually walking on the water until he looked around and noticed the wind and the waves. Then he began to sink. Likewise, when we go through troubled times, if we focus on the circumstances surrounding us, we too will become fearful and sink. But if we keep our eyes on Jesus and focus on His ability and willingness to carry us through, we will eventually come out on top. Notice that when Peter began to focus on the commotion about him, which caused him to sink, Jesus chided him for a lack of faith. While it's God who helps us to overcome our adversities, it's our faith that opens the door to receive His help.

LIVE ON PURPOSE TODAY

Sit quietly for a few minutes today to listen to what God is speaking to your heart.

But there's another interesting lesson for us here. Peter was the only disciple who had the courage to get out of the boat! Yes, he took his eyes off Jesus and began to sink as a result. Still, he was the only disciple to experience the miracle of walking on water with the Master. If you are going to do anything substantial for God, there are going to be times when He beckons you to get out of the boat and step out in faith. That means leaving your safety zone behind. It also means taking some risks. If you're waiting for the water to come inside the boat before you'll walk on it, you can forget it. God will not force you to get out of the boat. But if He calls and you don't answer, you will never know what awesome things He had planned for you. If you feel that the Lord is asking you today to step out in faith, tell Him you want His direction and timing, and ask Him to give you the courage you need to do His will. Then prepare to step out of the boat and into God's glory!

PRAYER

Lord, when I go through trials, help me to keep my eyes off my circumstances and on You. Hold me up and guide me safely through the storms of life. Whenever You call me to step out in faith, give me Your direction, discernment, and courage. Help me to be bold but not foolhardy. Help me to never jump ahead of Your plan or lag behind. Thank You for making me an overcomer and an instrument for Your glory!

The High Cost of Independence

You can never please God without faith,
without depending on him.

HEBREWS 11:6 TLB

Some years ago my husband, Joe, and I were planning to move to a larger home with our two growing sons. We were in the process of house hunting, when we discovered what appeared to be the perfect home at an irresistible price. Even though the house was already a bargain, my husband and I offered the seller much less than he was asking for, because we weren't sure we could afford the monthly payments any other way. A day or two later we discovered that we had lost our dream house to another buyer who outbid us. My family and I were devastated. Everything else we had seen in our price range paled in comparison to that house, and we held out little hope of finding another one like it. My father knew that Joe and I were in the market for a new home, so he was calling us regularly for updates. He happened to call the very night we lost our dream house, and when he asked how our search was going, I burst into tears and began telling him the whole sad story. To my surprise, my dad got angry and began scolding me. He wanted to know why I didn't come to him and ask him for help when I found the house that I wanted so badly. He chastised me for having an "independent spirit," and I realized then that my desire to do things on my own had hurt my father deeply. Before we got off the phone that night, my dad made me promise to call him as soon as Joe and I found another house we were interested in. Within the next few days we were able to find a lovely new home that we could afford with my father's help, and we promptly bought it.

Our original "dream house" is only about a mile away from the home we ended up buying. I pass it quite often, and I can't help wondering what it would have been like to live there with my family. These days it has become to me a reminder of what it can cost me when I neglect to ask for help when I have a need. My dad was right when he accused me of having an independent spirit. More than anything I wanted to do things *my* way—*myself.* And I wasn't alone. Most of the people I knew felt the same way. The only problem was that whenever we did do things our way and on our own, we usually didn't like the results. That's exactly why, when the Lord got my attention and invited me to surrender my life to Him, I was ready to try something drastic. I discovered that the more I yielded to Him and His ways, the more freedom, victory, and blessings I experienced. As I left my independent attitude behind and began living a life totally dependent upon God, my burdens lifted, and I began to experience the abundant life that Jesus spoke about. I found that one of the most important aspects of living God's way was to continually ask for His help—in little matters, as well as big ones. I soon discovered that my heavenly Father was even more eager to help than my

LIVE ON PURPOSE TODAY

What areas of your life are you trying to handle on your own? Your finances? Your health? Your family? Your job search? Ask God to help you be dependent on Him in that area.

earthly dad was. And I began to sense that my Father in heaven was even more deeply hurt than my dad when I neglected to ask for His help.

The Bible says, "You do not have because you do not ask" (James 4:2 NKJV). If I had only asked my dad to help us buy that first house, my family and I would be living in it now. Instead, I allowed my stubborn pride and my independent attitude to rob me of God's best. Jesus said, "If you, then, though you are evil, know how to give good gifts to your children, how much more will your Father in heaven give good gifts to those who *ask* Him!" (Matt. 7:11). If my earthly dad was so ready and willing to give good things to me and my family, how much more does our heavenly Father long to shower us with His abundant blessings? We can discover the answer for ourselves each time we do our part and *ask*, as Jesus says. If you, too, have been guilty of having an "independent spirit," I urge you not to pay the high cost of this attitude one more day. Instead, choose a life of dependence upon God, and begin asking Him for the abundant blessings He has in store for you!

PRAYER

Lord, forgive me for wanting to do things my own way, instead of Your way. Help me to realize that when I fail to seek Your help on a daily basis, I am not only hurting myself, but I am hurting You. Deliver me from an independent spirit, and teach me to rely on You more and more. Thank You that my dependence upon You will open the door to a greater level of victory and blessing!

Encouragement
for the Faithful

"Yet I reserve seven thousand in Israel—all whose knees have not bowed down to Baal and all whose mouths have not kissed him."

1 KINGS 19:18

These comforting words were spoken by God to the great prophet Elijah. At the time Elijah was feeling sorry for himself and lamenting the fact that he was the only one left in Israel who was true to God. The Lord sets the prophet straight by reassuring him that a faithful remnant still exists in the land, and Elijah is not alone.

I often hear from believers who are feeling downhearted and discouraged because of all the people around them who profess to be Christians but who are living carnal, worldly lives. If you're one of these faithful ones, I have some encouraging news for you today. Just like there existed a faithful remnant in Elijah's time, there exists one today. The apostle Paul writes about it in Romans 11:2-5, where he says, "So too, at the present time there is a remnant chosen by grace" (v. 5).

Even though we are not alone in serving the Lord faithfully, we will *feel* alone sometimes. That's when we need to heed some practical advice from the Bible so that we won't lose heart or be tempted to backslide. The author of Hebrews writes, "Let us run with perseverance the race marked out for us. Let us fix our eyes on Jesus, the author and perfecter of our faith" (Heb. 12:1,2). If we don't keep our eyes on the Lord, and if we let our eyes shift to focusing on other believers—especially carnal ones—we can risk becoming doubtful and

LIVE ON PURPOSE TODAY

Memorize Hebrews 12:1-2 NASB and confess it daily.

discouraged. That's exactly what the enemy of our souls, Satan, wants. He will parade all kinds of Christians before us who are living sloppy lives. And he will try to convince us that the Christian life is simply too hard and that God is expecting too much from us. Yes, it's true that trying to live a Christlike life can be hard. But those of us who have learned the hard way could attest to the fact that living our lives apart from Christ is even harder. Besides that, God has given us the Holy Spirit so that we can follow Jesus and become more like Him each day, as we devote ourselves to Him and His Word.

You may feel like you're the only believer who is suffering and feeling depressed right now, but you are not. I know exactly how you feel. And I'm urging you, in the words of the apostle Peter, to "remember that Christians all over the world are going through the same kind of suffering you are" (1 Peter 5:9 NLT). You are not alone in this fight. Countless other faithful believers are standing alongside of you, and I'm one of them. That's why I encourage you today to "take your share of suffering as a good soldier of Jesus Christ, just as I do, and as Christ's soldier, do not let yourself become tied up in worldly affairs, for then you cannot satisfy the One who has enlisted you in His army" (2 Tim. 2:3,4 TLB). Remember this—if you focus on the misbehavior of other Christians, you will live a life of frustration and mediocrity, and you will never be able to do much for God. But if you will keep your eyes fixed on Jesus, you will live a life of excellence and abundance, reaping earthly and heavenly blessings that are reserved exclusively for God's faithful ones!

PRAYER

Lord, forgive me for the times I've gotten distracted and discouraged by the behavior of other Christians. I pray that from now on their conduct will create in me a new resolve to devote myself to You and Your ways more and more. Thank You that my continued faithfulness will prove Your promises true!

Nothing's Too Hard for Him

See how the siege ramps are built up to take the city. Because
of the sword, famine and plague, the city will be handed over to
the Babylonians who are attacking it. What you said has
happened, as you now see. And though the city will be handed
over to the Babylonians, you, O Sovereign Lord, say to me,
"Buy the field with silver and have the transaction witnessed."
Then the word of the Lord came to Jeremiah: "I am the Lord,
the God of all mankind. Is anything too hard for me?"

JEREMIAH 32:24-26

G od revealed to Jeremiah, His faithful prophet, that the
Babylonians would conquer his nation and take his people
captive. That was the bad news. The good news was that
after a period of captivity, God would bring the people back to
their homeland, where they would rebuild and prosper once again.
Though Jerusalem is already surrounded, the Lord instructs
Jeremiah to purchase a nearby field from his uncle. It must have
been difficult for the prophet to publicly buy land which seemed
like such a poor investment to everyone, but Jeremiah obeyed
God. After he does, he is filled with doubt and turns to God in
prayer for reassurance. It is then that the Lord reminds him that
He is the God of the impossible.

Why did God have Jeremiah buy land at a time when
Jerusalem was under siege by the Babylonians? He wanted the
prophet to focus, not on the trials at hand, but on God's promise
of restoration for the future. Jeremiah's purchase was an act of

LIVE ON PURPOSE TODAY

On a small piece of paper or card write down your favorite promise verse. Put this in a place where you will see it on a daily basis: on your computer, on your mirror, on your refrigerator. Every time you see it say it out loud.

faith in God's promise. Perhaps today you're in a trial of your own and you're having doubts about God fulfilling His seemingly impossible promises to you. If so, I pray that you will be inspired by Jeremiah's example. God expects a lot from His children. He often asks us to demonstrate our trust in Him even when it seems that we are up against insurmountable odds. But let me reassure you today that if it takes a miracle for the Lord to fulfill His promises to you, our God is able and He will do it. Today, God is asking you—"Is anything too hard for Me?" If you can honestly answer Him, "No, Lord!" then your miracle is on its way!

PRAYER

Lord, I thank You for all Your great and precious promises. I ask that You increase my measure of faith so that I'll be able to trust You even in the most difficult times. When I'm tempted to doubt, remind me that nothing is too hard for You. Help me to keep my eyes on Your promises instead of my problems. Thank You for Your faithfulness!

Handling Finances God's Way

Of what use is money in the hand of a fool,
since he has no desire to get wisdom?

PROVERBS 17:16

A few years ago, when I became serious about getting out of debt, the Lord began showing me this verse. While it was His desire for me to live free from burdensome debt, He wasn't inclined to give me much help until I got serious about seeking His wisdom for handling my finances. He taught me a few things that have made all the difference, and I'd like to share them with you.

First, we have to seek God's wisdom and His will concerning our finances. If there's something we want—like a newer car or a vacation—we need to consult Him before we decide to take action. If we're not sure we have the Lord's permission, we need to wait on Him. And waiting on God is the second important thing He taught me. Each time I buy something on credit without God's approval, I forfeit the opportunity for Him to provide it for me debt-free. I've gotten to the point where I'm willing to wait on God for things if it means I can eventually pay cash for them. When you're serious enough about getting out of debt to do that, God will work wonders in your finances. Third, we need to trust God's provision. He has promised to abundantly supply all our needs (Phil. 4:19), and when we don't trust Him to do so, He takes it personally. God doesn't want us panicking when unexpected expenses come up. He also doesn't want us to be materialistic or self-indulgent. God wants to indulge us from time to time, but only if we don't continually indulge ourselves. Jesus told us to seek first God's kingdom and righteousness, and then He would supply our material needs. (Matt.

LIVE ON PURPOSE TODAY

Take the following action steps concerning your financial situation today:

1. Seek God's wisdom and will
2. Wait on God's timing
3. Trust God's provision

6:33.) He also equated those who seek things with pagans. The bottom line is that believers are not to seek things—we are to seek God. Then God will meet all our needs.

In addition, I believe it's very important for us to reach out to others with our material resources. The Bible says that "God loves a cheerful giver" (2 Cor. 9:7). And that when we sow generously—blessing others, we will reap generously—and with blessings. (2 Cor. 9:6 AMP.) God is much more likely to be generous toward us when we are generous toward others. Also, the Lord wants us to be content with what He's already given us. Hebrews 13:5 says, "Keep your lives free from the love of money and be content with what you have, because God has said, 'Never will I leave you; never will I forsake you.'" Often God will not bless us with something like a newer car until we are sincerely thankful for the one we already have. Being content with our possessions shows we are truly grateful for them. If you've made some mistakes with your finances, confess poor stewardship to the Lord and ask Him to help you be the steward He wants you to be. And know that God means it when He says, "Those who seek the Lord lack no good thing"! (Ps. 34:10).

PRAYER

Lord, forgive me for poor stewardship, and make me the steward You want me to be. Help me to always seek Your wisdom and Your perfect timing for all my expenditures. Make me a cheerful and generous giver, and teach me to be content with the blessings You've already given me. Thank You that because You're my Shepherd, I'll always have everything I need! (Ps. 23:1 TLB.)

Take Heart—
You Are Not Alone

Do not be afraid, for I have ransomed you. I have called
you by name; you are mine. When you go through deep
waters and great trouble, I will be with you. When you go
through rivers of difficulty, you will not drown! When you
walk through the fire of oppression, you will not be burned up;
the flames will not consume you. For I am the Lord,
your God, the Holy One of Israel, your Savior.

ISAIAH 43:1-3 NLT

These are just a few of the verses in the Bible that let us know that we can expect to go through some difficult times while we're on this earth. The good news is, though, that God will be with us so that we will not have to go through them alone. Some Christians seem to think that we shouldn't have to experience trials in this life and that we should expect God to spare us from them all. Then there are those believers who think that we shouldn't pray for protection or deliverance from suffering, because it's our lot in life to suffer. But the Bible is filled with numerous accounts of God miraculously delivering His people from all kinds of tribulations. It's also filled with promises of protection for believers. Just take a look at Psalm 91, one of the most quoted Bible passages of all time. As children of God we have the privilege, even the obligation at times, to pray for protection from evil and harm—not just for ourselves, but for others. While prayers like these will not always be answered the way we expect, we will always be worse off without them.

LIVE ON PURPOSE TODAY

Invite Jesus into your day today. Talk to Him just like you talk to your friends or family. You are not alone; He is always with you.

It is my heartfelt prayer that you would be spared from all difficulties in this life. But since that's not very likely, let me encourage you with some promises from God's Word which will reassure you that God will not abandon you during these times. Psalm 23:4 says, "Even though I walk through the valley of the shadow of death, I will fear no evil, for you are with me; your rod and your staff, they comfort me." David knew the Lord would never forsake him in times of trouble, and neither will He forsake you. In John 16:33 TLB, Jesus warns us to expect difficult times while we're here, and at the same time, He comforts us: "Here on earth you will have many trials and sorrows; but cheer up, for I have overcome the world." If you are in a trial today, please know that God has not left you alone in your time of need. If you are in doubt, ask Him to reveal Himself and His unfailing love for you. You may be surprised how quickly He answers that prayer. Let me encourage you today with Psalm 34:19 TLB: "The good man does not escape all troubles—he has them too. But the Lord helps him in each and every one"!

PRAYER

Lord, sometimes when I go through difficult times I feel so alone and helpless. At those times I ask that You wrap Your arms of love around me and comfort me the way only You can. Let me feel Your presence in a special way, and lift me above my circumstances. Thank You that You will never leave me nor forsake me!

Darkest Before Dawn

Do not, therefore, fling away your fearless confidence, for it carries a great and glorious compensation of reward. For you have need of steadfast patience and endurance, so that you may perform and fully accomplish the will of God, and thus receive and carry away [and enjoy to the full] what is promised.

HEBREWS 10:35,36 AMP

I recently read a story about a famous Russian writer who was imprisoned because of his religious convictions. The conditions in the labor camp he was in were so intolerable that he eventually began to contemplate suicide. When he realized that his faith in God would not allow it, he began formulating a plan of escape that would cause him to be shot by the prison guards. Without being told about the writer's intentions, a fellow inmate approached him and drew a cross on the ground. Acknowledging that it was a message from God, the writer abandoned his plan of escape and entrusted himself to the Lord. What he didn't know was that people all over the world were praying for his freedom, and just three days later he was released from prison.

Maybe you've heard the old saying "It's always darkest before the dawn." I believe that statement often holds true. It certainly did in the case of the Russian writer. It's no coincidence that right before his deliverance came, the temptation for him to lose faith in God became unbearable. These are the kinds of tactics that Satan uses to try to convince believers to abandon their faith and hope in God so that their victory will be delayed or even thwarted entirely. That's why the Bible says, "Do not throw away this confident trust in the Lord, no matter what happens. Remember the great reward it brings you! Patient endurance is what you need now, so you will continue to do God's will. Then you will receive all that he has promised" (Heb. 10:35,36 NLT). The devil knows that if he can send enough discouragement and despair your way, you'll be more likely to quit and give up on trusting in God and His plans for you. A few years ago I began making little notations in my Bible each time the Lord spoke an encouraging verse or promise to me in my times of trouble. These notes reveal that in many cases, right before my breakthrough came, the devil broke out his heaviest artillery in an attempt to pressure me to take my eyes off of God and to put them on my circumstances. Sometimes, like in the Russian writer's case, there were only a few days between my deepest despair and my deliverance. If that man had been aware of his imminent release, he would not have been so tempted to abandon his confidence in God. But he *didn't* know. And you and I

LIVE ON PURPOSE TODAY

Name one thing that you should be trusting God for. Tell Him that you are going to trust Him in that area. As you stand on His promises, watch how God comes through for you.

usually don't know, either. The Lord often chooses to do His work on our behalf behind the scenes. By doing things this way, He stretches and builds our faith and trust in Him, and He prepares us for the blessings and promotions He has in store for us. For me, the thing that stands out most about this man's story is the price he would have paid if he had stopped trusting God. He would have lost his life and missed out on witnessing God's awesome rescue operation on his behalf. What will it cost *you* if you fail to trust God in the hard places you're in right now? It's my sincere hope that you will "settle down and trust God," as the Russian writer did that fateful day. Who knows? Your deliverance could be only three days away.

PRAYER

Lord, when I'm tempted to cast away my confidence in You and Your perfect plans for me, remind me of how high the cost to me could be. Increase my trust in You daily, and help me to do my part by seeking You with all my heart. Thank You for the rich rewards my faithfulness will bring!

Believe and Receive

Against all hope, Abraham in hope believed and so became the father of many nations, just as it had been said to him, "So shall your offspring be." Without weakening in his faith, he faced the fact that his body was as good as dead—since he was about a hundred years old—and that Sarah's womb was also dead. Yet he did not waver through unbelief regarding the promise of God, but was strengthened in his faith and gave glory to God, being fully persuaded that God had power to do what he had promised.

ROMANS 4:18-21

These verses are a great encouragement to those of us who have ever had to endure long periods of waiting before we saw the fulfillment of God's promises to us. The emphasis here is upon the fact that Abraham's situation was completely hopeless. Yet he believed God's promise to give him a son in his old age. It was many years before God fulfilled this promise to Abraham, and he made some mistakes during those years. Still, these verses don't mention Abraham's doubts but focus instead on his faith. That fact should encourage us, too. Though we may struggle with our own doubts from time to time, if we hold on to God's promises, we will receive our reward just as Abraham did.

If you are not feeling very hopeful today that God's promises to you will ever come to pass, I urge you to hold on to your faith. Look at these verses in Hebrews 10:35-36 NLT: "Do not throw away this confident trust in the Lord, no matter what happens. Remember the great reward it brings you! Patient endurance is what you need now, so you will continue to do God's will. Then you will receive all that He has promised." If you throw your faith away before God fulfills

His promises to you, you will never receive the reward He has waiting for you. Ask the Lord to give you the patience and endurance you need to stand strong, then do your part by hanging in there when the going gets tough. Hebrews 6:12 TLB says, "Be anxious to follow the example of those who receive all that God has

LIVE ON PURPOSE TODAY

Whether you feel like it or not, whether your faith is on the brink of faltering or you are standing strong, lift your hands even now and offer thanksgiving and praise to the One who always keeps His promise of victory to those who trust Him.

promised them because of their strong faith and patience." Follow Abraham's example and receive all that the Lord has promised you. Not only will you be blessed, but God will be glorified through you, and then you can be an example to someone else whose faith is faltering. The Living Bible says that Abraham "praised God for this blessing even before it happened." If you'll begin thanking God right now for the fulfillment of those promises that look like they'll never come to pass, your faith will grow by leaps and bounds and you will delight the heart of God. Take heart from this precious verse in 2 Timothy 2:13 TLB: "Even when we are too weak to have any faith left, he remains faithful to us and will help us, for he cannot disown us who are part of himself, and he will always carry out his promises to us"!

PRAYER

Lord, whenever I'm tempted to doubt Your promises, increase my faith and give me the patience I need to stand strong. Help me to take my eyes off my circumstances and rest them on Your promises. Thank You for enabling me to receive all that You have promised!

Examining Our Motives

*People may be pure in their own eyes,
but the Lord examines their motives.*

PROVERBS 16:2 NLT

When my children were very young, their school used to sponsor an event each Christmas season that allowed the students to secretly shop for their family members and friends. The school asked for volunteers who would work in the shop and assist the children in making their selections and purchases. One year when I volunteered I worked with another mom who was obviously not very happy about doing her part. I inwardly cringed as she quickly became impatient with the kids, and seemed angry and resentful. I couldn't help but ask myself, "What is this woman doing here?"

Even though this incident happened many years ago, I can still remember it vividly. It's a constant reminder of how badly we can behave when our motives aren't right. I once heard a godly man say that if we can't walk in the fruit of the Spirit when we're involved with something, then maybe we should avoid it altogether. Did this woman think she was doing these kids a favor by being there that day? She certainly wasn't. I could tell by the looks on the children's faces that she was not being a blessing to them, but she was hurting them. Did the woman think she was doing God a favor by volunteering for something her heart wasn't in? Jesus made it clear that when we do even good deeds with wrong motives, we should not expect any reward from the Lord. (Matt.

6:1,2,16.) I don't know about you, but I certainly don't want anyone doing anything for me that they're going to resent doing. Isn't it likely that God feels the same way? The Bible says, "Love must be sincere" (Rom. 12:9). When we do things out of pure motives, we do them to *give*—not to *receive*. When we do things for others with an attitude that says—"What's in it for me?"—we are doing them with impure motives, and God is not pleased. The apostle Paul wrote, "Our purpose is to please God, not people. He is the one who examines the motives of our hearts" (1 Thess. 2:4 NLT). We may be able to hide our true motives from other people, but we will never be able to hide them from God. And even if we spend our entire lives doing good deeds, we will reap a bitter harvest if we did not do them with pure motives. On the other hand, if our purpose is to please God and not people, we will be more likely to only get involved with the things we can do with motives that will honor Him. David had the right idea when he prayed, "Put me on trial, Lord, and cross-examine me. Test my motives and affections" (Ps. 26:2 NLT). If we regularly examine our own motives behind the things we anticipate saying or doing, we may be able to avoid displeasing God and suffering the consequences that impure motives bring. And so, in the words of Jeremiah, I exhort you today—"Let us examine our ways and test them, and let us return to the Lord"! (Lam. 3:40).

LIVE ON PURPOSE TODAY

Take an inventory of your motives. Are you self-seeking? Do you desire to glorify God in everything? Memorize Psalm 51:10. Pray it daily for the next week and watch how God enters in and transforms your motives.

PRAYER

Lord, forgive me for the times I've done or said things out of impure motives. By the power of Your Spirit, please change me so that my purpose will always be to please and glorify You. Give me a heart that loves sincerely, and remove all phoniness from me. Thank You for helping me to examine my ways so that I can avoid the negative consequences of impure motives!

A Matter of Trust

It was so bad we didn't think we were going to make it.
We felt like we'd been sent to death row, that it was all over
for us. As it turned out, it was the best thing that could
have happened. Instead of trusting in our own strength or
wits to get out of it, we were forced to trust God totally—
not a bad idea since he's the God who raises the dead!
And he did it, rescued us from certain doom. And he'll do
it again, rescuing us as many times as we need rescuing.
You and your prayers are part of the rescue operation....

2 CORINTHIANS 1:8-11 MESSAGE

These verses penned by the apostle Paul have comforted countless believers over the ages because they remind us that when our circumstances look the bleakest, putting our trust in God can bring deliverance. Paul was a man of great faith, yet he admits here that he had doubts about his situation. He eventually comes to the point where he decides to put himself in the Lord's hands and "trust God totally." He then acknowledges God's infinite power and ability to breathe life into dead lives and circumstances. Nothing gives our God greater honor than putting our wholehearted trust in Him when we're going through difficult times. He in turn honors us by delivering us—often in miraculous ways. In Psalm 50:15 NLT, the Lord says, "Trust me in your times of trouble, and I will rescue you, and you will give me glory." When we go to God with our troubles and let Him know that we're depending on Him to deliver us, He puts His rescue operation in motion because He knows He'll get the glory for our deliverance. While it's true that walking through dark times can take their toll on us, we find a very encouraging biblical principle in the Book of Daniel. The prophet Daniel was thrown into a den of lions because he refused to worship anyone but the one true God. Even though Daniel did the right thing in remaining completely devoted to the Lord, he was not spared from having to endure a long night in a dark dungeon filled with hungry lions. But we discover that it was because of his faithfulness that he was miraculously delivered from certain destruction. Daniel 6:23 says, "And when Daniel was lifted from the den, no wound was found on him, because he had trusted in his God." Scripture makes it clear that it was Daniel's decision to put his trust in God that saved him. And just like Daniel came out of his trial unharmed, we can come out of our trials without any physical or emotional scars because of our faith in God.

LIVE ON PURPOSE TODAY

You have a need for intimacy with God. It is in your very nature. What are some areas in which you need to trust God more? Tell God how you are going to rely on Him in those areas.

What does the Bible say about putting our trust in someone other than God? Proverbs 28:26 says, "He who trusts in himself is a fool." The truth is, if we are not actively seeking God's help in our times of trouble, we are probably putting our trust in our own resources and abilities, and we will end up disappointed and defeated. Isaiah 2:22 NLT says, "Stop putting your trust in mere humans. They are as frail as breath. How can they be of help to anyone?" God warns us here not to make the mistake of depending on others to save us.

God wants to be our Savior, and He isn't about to let anyone else fill that role in our lives. And for those who are tempted to put their confidence in their finances, Proverbs 11:28 TLB warns, "Trust in your money and down you go!" The psalmist knew where to put his trust. Psalm 130:5 NLT says, "I am counting on the Lord; yes, I am counting on him. I have put my hope in his word." The Word of God can be our greatest source of encouragement and comfort when we're going through hard times. We can ask the Lord to give us a promise from His Word to cling to. In times of doubt, God's promises can give us the hope we need to stay focused on Him and His faithfulness, instead of on our circumstances. One way we can be certain that we've really placed our trust in God is that we will experience an indescribable peace. Isaiah 26:3 says, "You will keep in perfect peace all who trust in you, whose thoughts are fixed on you!" And Paul reminds us that the prayers of other believers can be "part of the rescue operation," so it's wise for us to ask God who we can turn to for prayer support. Let this promise from the Lord reassure you today: "None of those who have faith in God will ever be disgraced for trusting him"! (Ps. 25:3 TLB).

PRAYER

Lord, when I'm going through difficult times, help me to put my whole trust in You. Remind me that whenever I put my trust in myself or others, I will regret it in the end. Teach me to rely on Your Word for encouragement so that I won't be tempted to lose hope. Thank You that my faith in You will bring peace, joy, and victory!

No Condemnation

"Neither do I condemn you," Jesus declared.
"Go now and leave your life of sin."

JOHN 8:11

If you've ever struggled with guilt and condemnation as I have, the above verse is for you as much as it is for me. The apostle John records that when a woman caught in the act of adultery was brought before Jesus, instead of condemning her, He forgave her. During biblical times, according to Jewish law, people were stoned to death for this sin, so the Master's act of forgiveness here is truly remarkable. This passage should be a great comfort to all of us who have suffered the torment of guilt and condemnation after we've sinned. Jesus said, "Whoever believes in [Me] is not condemned, but whoever does not believe stands condemned already because he has not believed in the name of God's one and only Son" (John 3:18). And in John 5:24, Jesus says, "I tell you the truth, whoever hears my word and believes him who sent me has eternal life and will not be condemned; he has crossed over from death to life." These two statements make it clear that because we made the decision to put our faith in Christ and accept Him as our personal Savior, we will escape God's judgment and condemnation. We are not condemned because Jesus was condemned on our behalf on the cross. The apostle Paul states this in Romans 8:1 when he writes, "There is now no condemnation for those who are in Christ Jesus."

One thing we have to keep reminding ourselves is that God does not condemn the believer. While He gives us His Holy Spirit, whose job it is to convict us of sin so that we'll confess it and repent of it, the truth is that condemnation comes from Satan. In fact, the name *Satan* means "Accuser." Making the believer feel condemned is the devil's job, and he's very good at it. He knows that if he can make us feel condemned every time we falter, he can cause us to feel so hopeless and helpless that we'll never be able to live the victorious, fruitful life that Christ died to give us. Satan also wants to keep us feeling condemned because he knows it will make God seem distant from us, and this is one of his greatest deceptions. Yes, it should grieve our hearts when we sin, because sin grieves the heart of God. But the Lord doesn't want us wallowing in guilt and self-pity; He wants us to confess our sin, receive His forgiveness, ask for His help to overcome the sin, and then move on. Unlike confession and repentance, which are healing and constructive, condemnation immobilizes us and stunts our spiritual growth. It steals our joy and, therefore, our strength. (Neh. 8:10.) The Bible says that we should put on the whole armor of God each day so we can withstand the enemy's attacks. (Eph. 6:14-17.) This includes the breastplate of righteousness (which The Living Bible calls "the breastplate of God's approval") and the "sword of the

LIVE ON PURPOSE TODAY

Memorize 1 John 1:9.
Remind yourself when you have thoughts of guilt and condemnation that God has forgiven you!

Spirit, which is the word of God." Jesus defeated Satan with the written Word of God (Luke 4:1-13), and we must do the same. But we have to have a working knowledge of the Scriptures to do that. Psalm 119:11 says, "I have hidden Your word in my heart that I might not sin against You." The more we study and meditate on

God's Word, the more we will be able to resist sin and overcome Satan. The next time the devil tries to assail you with guilt and condemnation, remind him that you are the righteousness of God in Christ (2 Cor. 5:21), and the greater One lives in you (1 John 4:4)—and claim the victory that Jesus won for you! (1 Cor. 15:57.)

PRAYER

Lord, teach me to stand against the attacks of the enemy by continually acknowledging who I am in Christ and acting accordingly. Give me a love for Your Word so that I'll study and meditate on it till it gets deep in my heart and makes me a doer of the Word. When I do sin, help me to be quick to confess and repent, and remind me of Your promise to forgive and cleanse me. (1 John 1:9.) Thank You that my faith in Christ saves me from condemnation!

The Dangers of Higher Education

For with much wisdom comes much sorrow;
the more knowledge, the more grief.

ECCLESIASTES 1:18

These words were written by King Solomon, a man who was famous for his wisdom. After many years of striving to increase his wisdom and knowledge, he comes to the conclusion that the more he studies, the more miserable he becomes. To a society like ours, which is convinced that education is the answer for almost everything, these words may seem almost sacrilegious. In our pursuit of status and wealth, we have made education an idol. We have worshiped it, and we have used it to try to fill the void in ourselves which can only be filled with God. And where has all this education gotten us? It's left us empty and unfulfilled, living lives without purpose or meaning. It's also left many of us deeply in debt. We have begun to covet each other's levels of learning. We've become a society that feels it needs to "keep up with the Joneses" as far as degrees are concerned.

The Bible gives some clear warnings about placing too much value on education. Besides the verses above written by Solomon, Paul writes that "Knowledge puffs up, but love builds up" (1 Cor. 8:1). Too much education has a tendency to make us arrogant and prideful, and it can hinder our relationships with others and with God. In 1 Corinthians 3:18-19 NLT, Paul says, "Stop fooling yourselves. If you think you are wise by this world's standards, you will have to become a fool so you can become wise by God's standards.

LIVE ON PURPOSE TODAY

Our completeness comes from God, not our accomplishments. Take a minute to think about the education you have completed. No matter the level, you will never know as much as God. Thank Him for His wisdom and ask Him to give you more wisdom today.

For the wisdom of this world is foolishness to God." Paul was a highly educated man, yet he warns us here that striving to gain worldly wisdom can hinder us from accepting the wisdom from above which can save us. That's one of the reasons why Jesus said, "I tell you the truth, anyone who will not receive the kingdom of God like a little child will never enter it" (Luke 18:17). Children have a tendency to be humble and dependent, while highly educated people often demonstrate more arrogant and self-reliant attitudes. So what are Christians to do about their education? It's simple. Seek God. Then you'll get only the amount of education you really need, and He will provide the finances and the grace you need to excel in your schoolwork. He'll even open doors of opportunity when the time comes. Today, rest on this promise from God, penned by David in Psalms: "...In all my years I have never seen the Lord forsake a man who loves him; nor have I seen the children of the godly go hungry. Instead, the godly are able to be generous...and their children are a blessing"! (Ps. 37:25,26 TLB).

PRAYER

Lord, I ask today that You show me what education or training I need so that I may prepare to fulfill my God-given purpose. Give me Your plan for my life and don't let me get sidetracked with my own plans or those of others. Thank You for providing all that I need to be all that You want me to be!

The Power of Our Words

> *Death and life are in the power of the tongue, and they who indulge in it shall eat the fruit of it [for death or life].*
>
> PROVERBS 18:21 AMP

The verses above, and many other Scriptures in the Bible, reveal that our words have tremendous power. We can speak life to ourselves and others, or we can speak death. If you need some convincing that this is true, look at what the apostle Paul writes in Romans 10:9: "If you confess with your mouth, 'Jesus is Lord,' and believe in your heart that God raised him from the dead, you will be saved." Our words carry so much weight that they can even affirm our salvation and, therefore, affect the spiritual realm. Jesus warned us about taking our speech too lightly. In Matthew 12:36-37, He says, "But I tell you that men will have to give account on the day of judgment for every careless word they have spoken. For by your words you will be acquitted, and by your words you will be condemned."

To be honest, it disturbs me to hear so many believers say things like, "The flu is going around, and I just know I'm going to get it. I always do!" Or, "My son drives like a maniac. It's just a matter of time before he kills himself or somebody else!" Or even, "My parents fight all the time. They're definitely going to get a divorce!" I believe with all my heart that this kind of talk grieves the heart of God. Hebrews 11:6 says that "without faith it is impossible to please God." What kind of faith are we demonstrating when we speak words of doom and destruction over our children, or someone's marriage? Shouldn't we be praying and standing on God's

LIVE ON PURPOSE TODAY

In the intensity of a moment or situation you may have said some things that you now regret. Take a minute to repent for what you said and think about what you could have said instead. Use God's Word as a directive.

promises for them instead? And when we say that we are certain to become victims of illness, aren't we putting more faith in that affliction than in God's ability and willingness to keep us well or heal us? Wouldn't we be much wiser—and wouldn't God be more pleased—if we prayed in faith for God's protection and healing? Knowing that our words can affect the spiritual realm, isn't it likely that when we're speaking words of sickness, destruction, and defeat, that we're opening doors for the Destroyer to come in and attack us and our loved ones? Our words are seeds, and it's up to us whether we plant seeds of life or death. If we want to reap the right kind of harvest, then we've got to plant the right kind of seeds. I can tell you from experience that if you will change your words, you will change your life, and you will even affect those around you. May David's prayer be ours today: "May the words of my mouth and the thoughts of my heart be pleasing to You, O Lord, my Rock and my Redeemer" (Ps. 19:14 NLT).

PRAYER

Lord, forgive me for the times my speech has been filled with doubt and destruction instead of faith and life. Cleanse my lips the way You did Isaiah's. (Isa. 6:6,7.) Help me to speak words that please You and bless others. Remind me of all Your precious promises of wholeness, life, and victory. Thank You that my words of life will bring people hope and healing!

Forget the Results

> *"Master, we've worked hard all night and haven't caught anything. But because you say so, I will let down the nets."*
>
> LUKE 5:5

The Lord has used this verse many times to encourage my heart when I've been faced with disappointing results from my hard work. I can really relate to poor Peter here when, after fishing all night and catching nothing, the Lord asks him to let down his net one more time. It's as if Peter is saying, "Lord, I've worked hard and long, but I have nothing to show for it!" The only thing that motivates Peter to drop that net again is the Lord's command. As a result of his obedience, Peter is rewarded with a catch of fish that begins to break his nets and sink two boats. The disciple could have let his weariness and discouragement rob him of a miracle, but fortunately, he put his feelings aside and obeyed the Lord.

I think it's sad how our society has become so result-oriented. Too often we're initially excited about a new assignment that the Lord gives us, but as soon as we realize we aren't getting the results we expected, we quit and give up. And it *is* tempting to give up when we're not getting the results we want. I experienced this for myself several years ago, when my son started a Bible club in his public high school. After the initial excitement began to wear off, my son and I were tempted to "throw in the towel." We were working long and hard, and instead of the club growing in number, it was diminishing. It seemed like resistance was coming against us from all directions—including from some of the school authorities, teachers, and students. We wrestled with that quitter's attitude that says,

LIVE ON PURPOSE TODAY

Write down some goals.
Don't get discouraged if they
seem impossible right now.
Pray the prayer above and
commit your goals to God.

"Who needs this?!" Then the Lord spoke to our hearts. He told us not to worry about the results or the numbers. He told us to just be there for the kids that showed up, even if it was just a handful. And He told us to pray. If only two people came, they could pray and expect Jesus to be in their midst, like He promised. We made the decision that we were in it for the long haul. We stuck it out and didn't let our discouragement talk us out of doing God's will. It paid off big time. The club grew, and over a period of five years it touched and changed the lives of hundreds of kids. The fact is that when God gives us a job to do, even if it's just to pray or witness to someone, He doesn't want us focusing on the results. Yes, there will be times when it seems like we have nothing to show for our hard work. But if we obey God and keep going, the day will come when we'll be rewarded with a net-breaking, boat-sinking catch of our own. Be encouraged by this promise from God today: "Let us not get tired of doing what is right, for after a while we will reap a harvest of blessing if we don't get discouraged and give up"! (Gal. 6:9 TLB).

PRAYER

Lord, when You give me a job to do, help me not to focus on the results. Help me, instead, to focus on You and Your will. When it seems like I have nothing to show for my work, send me the encouragement I need to keep going. As I'm faithful, use me to touch and change more and more lives. Thank You for the harvest of blessings I'll reap!

Faith Is Spelled "R-I-S-K"

These were all commended for their faith, yet none
of them received what had been promised.

HEBREWS 11:39

It always amazes me how many believers are hesitant to claim
God's promises because they're afraid they'll be disappointed.
Perhaps they feel that if they don't expect too much from God,
they can avoid the pain of being let down. I've heard it said that
real faith is spelled "R-I-S-K." I think there's a lot of truth to that.
It takes a lot of courage to trust God to come through for us when
our senses aren't giving us any support. But that's exactly what
the Lord expects from us. If you look at the eleventh chapter of
Hebrews, you see that God approves of those who put their faith
in His promises, whether or not they come to pass. The verse
above confirms this. And so does Hebrews 11:13: "All these
people were still living by faith when they died. They did not
receive the things promised; they only saw them and welcomed
them from a distance." The Scriptures reveal that God holds in
high esteem those who live by faith and continue to hold on to
God's promises, even through long periods of waiting. The fact is,
if we really want to please God and reap the rewards He has in
store for us, we're going to have to risk putting our faith and trust
in Him, even when it looks like the odds are against us. Hebrews
11:6 tells us, "Without faith it is impossible to please God,
because anyone who comes to Him must believe that He exists,
and that He rewards those who earnestly seek Him."

The first verse of Hebrews gives us a biblical definition of faith: "Now faith is being sure of what we hope for and certain of what we do not see." And the next verse reveals that it's this kind of faith that God esteems: "This is what the ancients were commended for" (Heb. 11:1,2). The words "sure" and "certain" make it clear that faith is a confidence in God and His Word, even when we don't see any tangible evidence to justify that faith. And the verse that follows reveals why our believing in what we don't see isn't just "pie in the sky": "By faith we understand that the universe was formed at God's command, so that what is seen was not made out of what was visible" (Heb. 11:3). The Creator of the universe isn't the least bit hindered when our circumstances look "impossible." Making something out of nothing is what our God does best. Now you need to ask yourself how serious you are about pleasing God. If you're really serious, you aren't going to be able to avoid taking risks with your faith. Yes, you're going to experience some disappointments you might have escaped. But I guarantee you this— you're going to witness some miracles in your life that you would have otherwise missed. Hebrews 11:33 tells us that "through faith" some of God's people "gained what was promised." The bottom line is this—

LIVE ON PURPOSE TODAY

Apply your faith to any need you face today. Find a Scripture that promises your answer, take hold of it by faith, and then thank God for His gracious supply. Give God the opportunity to do what He does best— and make something out of nothing for you!

whether or not we receive all the promises we believe God for isn't the issue; the issue is whether or not we are living by faith, trusting God with all our hearts in every circumstance every day of our lives. When we do, along with God's hearty approval, we'll have a peace and joy in our hearts that will enable us to live the abundant life that Jesus came to give us. Today, my heartfelt prayer for you is that you'll *dare to believe!*

PRAYER

Lord, forgive me for the times I've missed Your perfect will because I was fearful or timid. Give me a holy boldness that will dare to believe in Your promises and to risk disappointment. Help me to keep my eyes on You and Your Word, instead of on my circumstances. Thank You that as I live by faith each day, I'll impact the lives of others with my peace and joy!

No Easy Way Out

For God did not give us a spirit of timidity
(of cowardice, of craven and cringing and fawning fear), but
[He has given us a spirit] of power and of love and of calm
and well-balanced mind and discipline and self-control.

2 TIMOTHY 1:7 AMP

When I went to the dentist recently to have some work done on a broken tooth, the temporary cap that he placed in my mouth was very uncomfortable. I was reluctant to tell my dentist about it because I was a new patient and I really didn't want to complain. So I pleaded with the Lord and asked Him to remove the pain and discomfort. As I prayed, I got the distinct impression that God wanted me to confront my dentist about it. After an unsettling night I called my dentist's office and asked for an appointment for that same day. As I sat in the waiting room reading a magazine, I came upon an article urging patients to be completely honest with their doctors about their true concerns. I was certain that this was confirmation from the Lord, and I asked Him to give me the strength, the courage, and the words I needed to confront my dentist. As soon as he called me into his office, I gently but firmly shared my concerns and complaints with him, and he promptly corrected the problem so that I noticed an immediate improvement.

I believe that God used this experience to teach me yet another lesson about how important it is for me to face certain situations and people with openness and honesty. The Bible clearly states that we are not to let others intimidate us, but even so, I confess that there are times when I really struggle with this issue. And I'm not the only one. I know a lot of believers who have the same problem. Why does God frown on our being intimidated by people and situations? Because He knows that as long as we are being influenced by anyone or anything other than His Spirit, Satan can easily manipulate us and sidetrack us with things that are out of God's will for us. Many of us will be called by God to assume positions of authority. We can't expect Him to promote us to higher places until we've proven that we aren't going to be controlled by the plans and expectations of others. When the Lord promotes us, it's so that we can fulfill His purposes and please Him, not others or ourselves. And that should always be our focus.

The experience I shared with you wasn't exactly a monumental one, but I do believe that it was a test that God used to help me overcome some of the fears I've had all my life. Proverbs 29:25 TLB says, "Fear of man is a dangerous trap, but to trust in God means safety." I've learned that our fear of man can be so

LIVE ON PURPOSE TODAY

Men were created with the ability to face difficult times with boldness. Think about a time when you cowered instead of being bold. Don't let this discourage you. Learn from your mistake. God lives within you!

subtle that we don't even realize it exists in our lives. In order to avoid confronting others, we may try to justify or accept certain wrong situations or someone else's unacceptable behavior. We then resolve ourselves to tolerating something that God wants us to deal with. This avoidance is disobedience, and it will keep us from receiving God's best. The Bible says, "God did not give us a spirit of timidity, but a spirit of power, of love and of self-discipline" (2 Tim. 1:7). We are equipped with Holy Spirit power to supernaturally confront and overcome intimidating people and situations. But we need to exercise that ability and develop it daily through our everyday experiences. We can take great comfort in knowing that each time we make the decision to confront instead of run away, God will back us up with all the wisdom and strength we need to triumph over our anxieties and fears, and to gain the victory in our situation. In Matthew 10:20 TLB, the Lord promises, "You will be given the right words at the right time." That day when I was pleading with the Lord to grant me relief from my mouth pain, He made it clear that He wasn't going to give me an easy way out. Now I'm glad He didn't. He taught me a valuable lesson that day, and He gave me the opportunity to position myself for great blessing and promotion. The next time you're in a tight spot with no easy way out, make up your mind to obey the Lord and declare with the prophet Isaiah— "Because the Lord God helps me, I will not be dismayed; therefore, I have set my face like flint to do His will, and I know that I will triumph"! (Isa. 50:7 TLB).

PRAYER

Lord, please forgive me for the times that I took the easy way out instead of obeying You. Give me the wisdom and the courage I need to confront those people and situations You want me to deal with. Thank You for the joy, peace, and freedom I'll experience as a result!

Anger Vs. Assistance

Everyone should be quick to listen, slow to speak and slow to become angry, for man's anger does not bring about the righteous life that God desires.

JAMES 1:19,20

Last week I lent my cellular phone to my son when he was going out. This wasn't exactly unusual, but what was unusual was the fact that after he returned home and I asked him to replace it in the recharger, he confessed that he didn't know where it was. We immediately began searching for it in every place we could imagine. As our search failed to uncover my phone, I felt that old familiar feeling of blood rushing to my head. My anger and frustration were building. I was tempted to say something to my son that I knew I'd have to repent for later. At the moment I figured it might be worth it. Just then, God gave me a "knowing" that if I wanted His help, I needed to restrain my anger, pray, and leave the matter in His hands. As much as I wanted to vent my anger on my son, I wanted my phone back even more. So I told my son we would resume our search the following day and I went to bed, entrusting the matter to the Lord. The next day I told my husband about the missing phone. It only took him a minute or two to discover its location, and I knew it was God's way of teaching me about the importance of remaining calm and kind in the midst of turmoil.

The Bible says, "Keep your head in all situations" (2 Tim. 4:5). While it's the world's way to fly off the handle every time they feel like it, believers are gifted with Holy Spirit self-control (2 Tim. 1:7), and God expects us to make use of it in tense situations. At first glance it seems like worldly people have an unfair advantage because it's often easier to vent our anger, and it seems to make us feel better initially. But the truth is that the consequences these people suffer as a result of their unrestrained anger are ones that the Lord would rather spare us from. Ecclesiastes 7:9 says, "Do not be quickly provoked in your spirit, for anger resides in the lap of fools." And Proverbs 14:17 says, "A quick-tempered man does foolish things." Losing our cool will cause us to make mistakes in word and deed that we'll regret later on. It's just not worth it. Proverbs 15:18 NLT says, "A hothead starts fights; a cool-tempered person tries to stop them." Jesus has called us to be peacemakers (Matt. 5:9), and He has given us His Spirit so we have the ability and the desire to prevent and halt dissension, instead of contributing to it. One way we can do that is by saying the right thing at the right time. Proverbs 15:1 says, "A gentle answer turns away wrath, but a harsh word stirs up anger." Often we can deflect someone's anger by speaking words of gentleness and understanding. In cases like these, I've often whispered a silent prayer for help, claiming God's promise in Proverbs 16:1 AMP which says, "From the Lord comes the [wise] answer of the tongue." I used to think that I had to have the last word in situations like these if I wanted to come out on

LIVE ON PURPOSE TODAY

Think about a time when you lost control of your temper. What could you have done differently in that situation? When facing similar situations in the future, how will you handle them?

top. Now I know that it's often just the opposite. God has taught me that even if I appear to others to come out the loser, I will have won in His eyes, and He will reward me somehow. I think believers would be more motivated to resist anger if they knew how destructive it really is. Ephesians 4:26 NLT says, "Don't sin by letting anger gain control over you. Don't let the sun go down while you are still angry, for anger gives a mighty foothold to the devil." When we lose our temper, we may be opening the door for Satan to come in and "steal, kill and destroy" (John 10:10). That's why being patient is actually spiritual warfare. The next time you're in a tense situation, ask yourself which you want more— the "luxury" of venting your anger, or the rewards of God's help. I pray you'll choose the latter and discover for yourself that "a wonderful future lies before those who love peace" (Ps. 37:37 NLT).

PRAYER

Lord, show me how to cooperate with Your plan to develop more patience in me. Remind me that when I choose to lose my temper in a situation, I could be forfeiting Your help. When I do get angry, help me to "get over it quickly," as Your Word commands (Eph. 4:26 TLB). Thank You that by Your grace I'll be a peacemaker, instead of a troublemaker!

Do You Want To Get Well?

{ *When Jesus saw him lying there and learned that*
he had been in this condition for a long time,
He asked him, "Do you want to get well?" }

JOHN 5:6

Many times I've read the above words by Jesus and thought to myself, *Who wouldn't want to get well if they were hurting in some way?* That question was answered for me recently when I was having a phone conversation with a lady from my church. She was going through a very difficult time in her life, and she was having a hard time dealing with all the injustices that were being heaped upon her, seemingly all at one time. As we chatted it became clear to me that she was harboring a lot of bitterness and resentment toward all the people who she felt had done her wrong. When I reminded her that Jesus has commanded us to forgive those who offend us, she insisted that she had a right to be resentful, and that she had no intention of forgiving those who hurt her. When I suggested that there might be a connection between her recent health problems and her feelings of resentment, she said she didn't care. She also confessed that she was angry with God and that her troubles were not drawing her closer to Him, but only further away. I decided then to drop the subject and to commit myself to pray for her in a more earnest manner from then on.

Why is it that some people become bitter when they go through hard times, while others become better? Perhaps part of the answer lies in an old saying that still rings true today: "The same hot water that hardens an egg, softens a carrot." We don't always have a choice about what happens to us, but we do have the power to choose how we will respond to the difficulties that come our way. Because this woman chose to withhold forgiveness from those who wounded her, she had also made the choice to forfeit the valuable help the Lord would have given her if she had only obeyed Him. Jesus said, "If you do not forgive men their sins, your Father will not forgive your sins" (Matt. 6:15). Unforgiveness is serious business in God's eyes, and we need to view it the same way and act accordingly. Fortunately, we don't have to forgive others in our own strength. We have the Holy Spirit pouring the God-kind of love into our hearts as we walk with Him daily. (Rom. 5:5.) The apostle Paul warns us that withholding forgiveness from others can open the door to satanic attack. (Eph. 4:26-28.) Maybe this woman's recent health problems weren't a direct result of her resentment, but one thing was certain—her bitterness was hindering her prayers, including her prayers for healing. In at least two places in the Gospels, Jesus reveals a link between the effectiveness of our prayers and our obligation to forgive others. (Matt. 6:14,15; Mark 11:25.)

LIVE ON PURPOSE TODAY

Take a moment and ask God to bring healing to wounds you have from the past. The Holy Spirit will bring you comfort and restoration to the deepest part of you, no matter the offense.

Perhaps the Lord is asking you today, "Do you want to get well?" No matter what you've been through or how many emotional scars you've built up over the years, healing and restoration are available to you. All you need to do is stop focusing on your wounds and begin focusing on the cure. There is no pain, injury, or hurt that the love of God cannot heal. I'm living proof of that, and so are many others. Ask the Lord to search your heart and reveal to you who it is you need to forgive. Then leave all your bitterness, resentment, and unforgiveness at the foot of the Cross— and let the healing begin!

PRAYER

Lord, teach me how to forgive others quickly and thoroughly when they hurt me or treat me unfairly. Remind me that You are faithful to right the wrongs in my life and to heal and comfort me when I look to You for wisdom and help in these situations. Thank You, Lord, that by Your grace I will benefit from my troubles and trials, and I will become better instead of bitter!

Let Your Light Shine

You are the light of the world. A city on a hill cannot be hidden. Neither do people light a lamp and put it under a bowl. Instead they put it on its stand, and it gives light to everyone in the house. In the same way, let your light shine before men, that they may see your good deeds and praise your Father in heaven.

MATTHEW 5:14-16

At a family gathering a few years ago, I couldn't help overhearing a discussion between my son John and a friend of the family. They were talking about a movie that was currently in the theaters and had a soundtrack of popular songs. When my son voiced his disapproval of the album because one of the song titles was an obscenity, I heard this friend exclaim, "Lighten up, John!" What was this friend saying to my son? She was basically saying, "C'mon, John, stop being so serious—and start thinking the way the rest of us do!"

Why do some folks—Christians and non-Christians alike—get so indignant when someone like John takes a stand against the popular culture? It makes them feel uncomfortable. It's like shining a spotlight on their questionable behavior for all the world to see. Jesus said that He wanted His followers to be salt and light to the world around them. (Matt. 5:13-16.) Why? Because it's the only way we can make a real difference for God on this earth. The apostle Paul wrote, "Have nothing to do with the fruitless deeds of darkness, but rather expose them" (Eph. 5:11). Naturally, we can use words to expose the sin around us, but there's an even better way. We can expose the works of darkness by our actions. There's an old saying that goes like this: "People may not believe what you say, but they'll believe what you *do!*" When mere words don't have an impact on the people around us, our Christlike behavior often can. In the same passage of Scripture, Paul goes on to say, "But when the light shines on them, it becomes clear how evil these things are. And where your light shines, it will expose their evil deeds" (Eph. 5:13,14 NLT). Every time that you and I "go along with the flow" of popular culture, our light for Christ dims and we lose an opportunity to draw others to Him. That's one reason why Paul continues with, "Be very careful then, how you live—not as unwise but as wise, making the most of every opportunity, because the days are evil" (Eph. 5:15,16).

The following verse gets to the heart of the matter: "Therefore, do not be foolish, but understand what the Lord's will is" (Eph. 5:17). The only way we're going to be able to live a life that's pleasing to God, and one that will impact others for His kingdom, is to have a working knowledge of His Word. How did John know that the profane song title on that movie soundtrack was offensive to God? Because he was familiar with the Scripture that says, "But among you there must not be even a hint of sexual immorality, or of any kind of impurity, or of greed, because these are improper for God's holy people. Nor should

LIVE ON PURPOSE TODAY

All day long, be on the lookout for an opportunity to be a bold witness for Jesus Christ—a bold witness with a shining light. Allow your words and actions to uphold Bible standards even in a dark world.

there be obscenity, foolish talk or coarse joking, which are out of place, but rather thanksgiving" (Eph. 5:3,4). John didn't just have head knowledge of these verses, but he was applying them to his life and walking them out, instead of just talking about them. And people take notice. When John's at work and everyone around him is cursing and blaspheming, he refuses to join in. He doesn't hit people over the head with his Bible, but he lets his light shine through his words and actions. And he stands out in a crowd. Yes, there's a price to be paid when we live our lives for God. And there are untold sacrifices that we have to make daily. But the rewards far outweigh them all. Just ask John. Because of his faithfulness, the Lord is using him to touch the lives of millions of people each year for His glory. And if you were to ask my son, he'd tell you that he wouldn't want to live any other way. The next time you take a bold stand for the Lord and someone says to you, "Lighten up!"—don't forget that that's your cue to let your light shine!

PRAYER

Lord, give me the strength, the wisdom, and the courage I need to "go against the flow" of our worldly popular culture. Teach me how to devote myself to You and Your Word and to apply Your principles to my life so I can make a real difference for You. Thank You that as I take advantage of every opportunity that comes my way, You will use me to touch and change the lives of multitudes!

Not Perfect? Read This!

> *It is clear, then, that God's promise to give the whole earth to Abraham and his descendants was not because Abraham obeyed God's laws but because he trusted God to keep his promise. So if you still claim that God's blessings go to those who are "good enough," then you are saying that God's promises to those who have faith are meaningless, and faith is foolish. But the fact of the matter is this: when we try to gain God's blessing and salvation by keeping his laws we always end up under his anger, for we always fail to keep them. The only way we can keep from breaking laws is not to have any to break! So God's blessings are given to us by faith, as a free gift.*
>
> ROMANS 4:13-16 TLB

When I first saw these verses in the Bible, I underlined them and put stars all around them. Do you ever feel like you don't deserve God's gift of salvation? If you do, I know how you feel. These verses are for you as much as for me. They tell us that we don't have to earn salvation or God's love. We couldn't even if we wanted to. The truth is, we could never be "good enough" to save ourselves. That's exactly why God sent us a Savior. In fact, the Bible reveals that even our best efforts wouldn't measure up. Isaiah 64:6 says, "All our righteous acts are like filthy rags." But while we can't model perfection, we can model spiritual growth. Out of gratitude for God's gracious gift, we can seek to abide in Him and be fruitful for His glory. And we can serve Him and others out of a thankful heart.

In Ephesians 2:8-9, Paul writes, "For it is by grace you have been saved, through faith—and this not from yourselves, it is the gift of God—not by works, so that no one can boast." One reason why God wants to make our salvation a gift is so that we can't boast about it or take the credit for it. God wants the glory, and He deserves it. Scripture reveals that when people asked Jesus, "What must we do to do the works God requires?" He answered them, "The work of God is this: to believe in the one he has sent" (John 6:28,29). We all know how much Jesus spoke about the importance of our doing good works and loving and serving God, but here He gives us the bottom line. It's not what we do that matters most to God; it's in whom we believe. It's not what we do that makes us righteous in God's sight; it's what He has done for us. Does that mean that the Bible condones sin? Not at all. The same man who wrote the verses above in Romans 4, the apostle Paul, also wrote in Romans 6:2, "Shall we go on sinning so that grace may increase? By no means! We died to sin; how can we live in it any longer?" From the moment of salvation we are empowered by the Holy Spirit to resist sin and obey God. We become increasingly uncomfortable with sin, and God's ways become more attractive to us. And Scripture assures us that "God is at work within us,

LIVE ON PURPOSE TODAY

Write down Ephesians 2:8-9: "For it is by grace you have been saved, through faith— and this not from yourselves, it is the gift of God—not by works, so that no one can boast." Memorize it and remind yourself when thoughts of guilt and condemnation try to come.

helping us want to obey him, and then helping us do what he wants" (Phil. 2:13 TLB). I pray that these truths will help you to relax a little more and enjoy your special relationship with God. May you rest in this precious promise from Him: "So now, since we have been made right in God's sight by faith in his promises, we can have real peace with him because of what Jesus Christ our Lord has done for us"! (Rom. 5:1 TLB).

PRAYER

Lord, forgive me for trying to earn the salvation You want me to receive as a free gift. Help me to stop striving to please You and to learn to abide and rest in You. Give me a revelation of my new identity in Christ so that I can cooperate with Your plan for my spiritual growth. Thank You for showing me that it's not my perfection that counts, but Yours!

According to Your Faith

Then [Jesus] touched their eyes and said,
'According to your faith will it be done to you.'

MATTHEW 9:29

Maybe you've read the following imagined story of a scene in heaven. Some angels approach the throne and say, "Father, there is a mortal on earth asking for a blessing. What is Thy pleasure concerning his request?" The Father asks, "What did he send his faith in?" The angels answer, "He sent his faith in a thimble." The Father responds, "Well, fill the thimble with blessings and send it back to him. According to his faith, be it unto him." Again the angels come and say, "Father, another mortal is asking blessings of Thee." Again the Father inquires, "And what did he send his faith in?" The angels respond, "He sent his faith in a huge barrel." With a smile the Father says, "Fill the barrel with blessings and send it back to him. According to his faith, be it unto him."

Until I began seriously studying the Bible some years ago, I didn't know just how much of an impact my faith could have on my life and the lives of others. No one had ever told me that praying in faith, using my faith, and nurturing my faith were largely my responsibility. One of the verses that God used to begin opening my eyes to this truth is in Matthew 9:29 NKJV where Jesus says, "According to your faith let it be to you." The Savior spoke these words to two blind men who came to Him for healing, letting them know that the quality of their faith played a role in how the Lord responded to their request. The fact is that we *do* have a certain amount of control over our lives, and how we exercise our faith and trust in God *can* determine our outcome to some extent. While it's true that God *is* sovereign, He gives believers the awesome privilege of playing an important part in their own futures.

In addition, our faith and trust in God can make a tremendous difference in the lives of others. In Matthew 8:13, when Jesus said, "It will be done just as you believed it would," He was speaking to the centurion about the healing of his servant, not about the soldier's own healing, as in the case of the blind men. And in Mark 2:5 TLB, when four men brought their crippled friend to Jesus for healing, the Scripture says that the Savior healed the man "when Jesus saw how strongly they believed that He would help." I think it's interesting that the Bible doesn't reveal whether or not the ailing friend had faith for his own healing. It only talks about the faith of his friends, and apparently, that is what we're supposed to focus on. In Mark 9:20-24, when a distraught father comes to Jesus to ask for his son's healing, the Lord indicates that the man's faith will play a vital part in his son's fate. Jesus tells him, "Everything is possible for him who believes."

LIVE ON PURPOSE TODAY

Start building your faith up by believing God for little things first, such as a pair of socks. Once you receive the socks, believe God for something a little bigger. This may take a little time, but your faith will grow bigger and bigger each time.

We don't have to let these awesome truths intimidate us or make us fearful. Instead, we can thank God for making a way for us to make a major difference in our own lives and the lives of others. If it's your desire to have greater faith, ask the Lord to increase your faith daily. But don't stop there. Do your part by devoting yourself to God's Word—reading it, believing it, memorizing it, meditating on it, and obeying it. Before you know it, your faith will begin growing by leaps and bounds. And you'll begin experiencing more and more of the joy and satisfaction that come from bearing fruit for God's kingdom and glory. I heard a world-changing minister of the Gospel being interviewed one day. He was asked how he had accomplished so much for God. His answer was, "I always figured that if you've got a big God, you should ask Him for big things!" Don't play it safe with your faith. Start taking risks with it. The next time you have a need or seek a blessing from the Lord, don't send Him your faith in a thimble. Send it in a barrel overflowing with faith, knowing He'll return it to you overflowing with blessings!

PRAYER

Lord, it's my heart's desire to have great faith in You. I want not only to make a difference in my own life, but to touch and change the lives of others. Enable me to do that, Lord, and help me to do my part in the process. Thank You that my great and growing faith will bear an abundance of fruit for Your glory!

Grace Under Pressure

> *...Love your enemies, do good to those who hate you, bless those who curse you, pray for those who mistreat you.... Do to others as you would have them do to you.... If you love those who love you, what credit is that to you? Even 'sinners' love those who love them. And if you do good to those who are good to you, what credit is that to you? Even 'sinners' do that.*
>
> LUKE 6:27-28,31-33

Jesus makes it clear in these verses that He expects a lot from us, especially in the area of how we relate to others. Though it may be "natural" for us to respond to mistreatment with anger or hostility, we are called to live "supernatural" lives through the grace and power of the Holy Spirit living in us. Jesus is not impressed when we are good to those who are good to us, because even unbelievers are capable of doing that. But He expects us to do the right thing, even when the right thing is not being done to us. Jesus knew what it was like to be mistreated. He was kind, compassionate, and good, yet He was still persecuted wherever He went. And He warned His disciples that they could expect the same treatment. In John 15:18 and 20, Jesus tells us, "If the world hates you, keep in mind that it hated me first.... No servant is greater than his master. If they persecuted me, they will persecute you also." Knowing this, we have to decide if we are going to live our lives reacting like everyone else in these situations, or responding the way Jesus expects us to.

In Romans chapter 12, the apostle Paul teaches us how to respond to those who mistreat us. "Do not repay anyone evil for evil.... Do not take revenge, my friends, but leave room for God's wrath, for it is written: 'It is mine to avenge; I will repay,' says the Lord.... Do not be overcome by evil, but overcome evil with good" (vv. 17,19,21). It's God's job to judge others, not ours. If we take matters into our own

LIVE ON PURPOSE TODAY

If you have been mistreated, forgive the person who mistreated you. Take a moment to pray for them right now.

hands, we don't "leave room for God's wrath," and God may not intervene in the situation at all because we haven't given Him place. He may feel that our retaliation is punishment enough for the one who wronged us. But if we leave the matter in God's hands, though we are letting the person off the hook, he is not off God's hook, and He will deal with them. When we release the wrongdoer to God, we are not excusing his actions; we are just for-giving him as an act of obedience to God. Don't expect your feel-ings to help you. You have to do it as an act of your will, and you may have to do it by faith. Often our feelings will fall in line after we do the right thing. Today, God is calling you to a higher level of faith, obedience, and reward. Let me encourage you with a promise from His Word: "Let us not get tired of doing what is right, for after a while we will reap a harvest of blessing if we don't get dis-couraged and give up"! (Gal. 6:9 TLB).

PRAYER

Lord, forgive me for the times I haven't acted Christlike when I've been treated unfairly. Help me to remember that You've placed a higher calling on my life and You expect much more from me. When I am mistreated, give me Your guidance and grace so that I may respond the way You want me to. Thank You that my witness will lead others to You!

From Trials to Triumphs

About midnight Paul and Silas were praying and singing hymns to God, and the other prisoners were listening to them. Suddenly there was such a violent earthquake that the foundations of the prison were shaken. At once all the prison doors flew open, and everybody's chains came loose.

ACTS 16:25,26

Paul and Silas were thrown into prison in Philippi for casting a demon out of a young slave girl who had been earning her master a lot of money. The disciples were stripped, beaten, and chained in a cell. The next thing that happened still amazes me, no matter how often I read it in Scripture. Paul and Silas began to pray and praise God in song. Most of us would have been grumbling and drowning in self-pity. We might have said something like, "God, here I am trying to serve You and lead others to You. How could You let these people do this to me? I don't deserve this!" Fortunately, instead of complaining, these disciples praised God, who responded by miraculously setting His servants free from captivity. As a result, the jailer and his entire household became believers.

Perhaps you are in a trial of your own today. Maybe the last thing you feel like doing is praising God. But listen to what Scripture teaches us. David said in Psalm 34:1, "I will bless the Lord at all times; his praise shall continually be in my mouth." And he meant it. Whether David was experiencing good times or bad, he praised God. Just one example of this is in 2 Samuel

12:20, where David and Bathsheba's infant son has just died as part of God's chastisement of the couple. The first thing David does is "go into the house of the Lord and worship God." This is just one of the many reasons why God called David a man after His own heart. And though the Lord allowed His servant to suffer the consequences of his sins, He gave David victory over all his enemies and blessed him with great wealth and honor. Paul and Silas praised God in the darkest of circumstances and unbelievers turned to Christ. If you'll praise God in your trials, your example could very well attract the attention of those who won't be reached any other way. Not only that, but you may find that the Lord will turn your trials into triumphs!

LIVE ON PURPOSE TODAY

Whether you're experiencing an "up" or a "down"— and even if it's midnight in your circumstances—stop right now and offer up thanksgiving, praise, and worship to the Lord!

PRAYER

Lord, forgive me for the times I've grumbled and felt sorry for myself in times of trouble. I ask You to remind me that You deserve praise through all my ups and downs. Help me to realize how blessed I really am, and give me a thankful heart. Thank You that my example will change the lives of others for Your glory!

Good Things Vs. God Things

Teach me to do Your will, for You are my God;
may Your good Spirit lead me on level ground.

PSALM 143:10

Last year my husband and I joined a small Bible study group affiliated with our church. We were hesitant at first because our schedules were already crowded, but we felt led by the Lord to commit ourselves to this group, and we trusted God to make a way for us to attend. Even with all the challenges involved, the entire experience turned out to be a wonderful blessing to us. When the next group session began, my husband and I were even more hesitant than the first time to commit ourselves. The second session would coincide with tax season, which meant that Joe would be working a full-time job and running a small business besides. Even though we suspected we were making a mistake, we caved in to the pressure from the rest of the group, and we committed ourselves once again. This time I actually dreaded attending those meetings. My heart just wasn't in it like the first time. Not only was there no "life" in the meetings for me, but it aggravated me to see my husband wearing himself out trying to keep our commitment. After earnestly praying and seeking God, I called our group leader and tactfully but firmly told him that we would not be finishing out the second session of meetings. He was disappointed and tried to convince me to change my mind, but I held firm and he finally relented. Though I felt a little guilty afterwards, I also felt a great sense of relief, and I knew I had done the right thing.

This experience confirmed to me once again that when I get involved with something that God never meant for me to, it's usually a waste of time and energy. Maybe you've heard the saying, "Not every 'good' thing is a 'God' thing." In other words, there's no guarantee that everything "good" that we get involved with is God's will for us. In fact, one of Satan's most effective ploys is to try to get us sidetracked doing "good" things so that we won't be able to fulfill our God-given purpose. That's why it's so important for us to seek God each day through prayer and Bible study, maintaining an attitude that says, "God, what is *Your* will for me as far as this is concerned?" If we don't, we'll keep getting involved with things that God never meant for us to simply because someone talked us into them, or because we think we "should." What usually happens then is that we end up hating our involvement, and we get little value or satisfaction out of it.

Besides that, our efforts will most likely drain us, instead of lift us up and edify us. And because we don't have a "right heart" about the whole thing, we can't expect God to reward us for it, even though it may be benefiting others. I made a big mistake in assuming that just because my group experience was so right

LIVE ON PURPOSE TODAY

Reflect today upon your current commitments and various activities, and determine which are "good" things" and which are "God" things. Don't hesitate to set change in motion, as the Holy Spirit leads.

for me the first time, it would be the same for me again. God doesn't want us being led by our past experiences, but by His Spirit. He also doesn't want us being led by other people. Just because God might have led the others in my group to join a second session, I shouldn't have assumed that this was His will for me. Even if everyone else in my group experienced an abundance of blessings as a result of their involvement, that's no guarantee that the same would be true in my case. It's only when we are where God wants us to be that we experience the fullness of His blessings. In the Psalms, David prayed, "Teach me to do Your will, for You are my God; may Your good Spirit lead me on level ground" (Ps. 143:10). While we should always have an attitude that seeks to do good, our main focus should not be on doing good things, but on doing God's will for us. Maintaining an attitude like this will take a lot of pressure off of us and enable us to walk in the freedom that God wants us to enjoy. The next time you're faced with an opportunity to do something good, don't just assume that it's God's will for you. Instead, pause long enough to ask for His wisdom and guidance in the matter, making certain that it's not just good—but God!

PRAYER

Lord, teach me how to avoid getting involved with things
that are not Your best for me. Show me how to seek You
continually and to be led by Your Spirit. Thank You, Lord,
that as I follow You daily, my life will be fulfilling and fruitful!

Faithful in Little Things

He who is faithful in a very little thing is faithful also in much.

LUKE 16:10 NASB

Unless you are faithful in small matters,
you won't be faithful in large ones.

LUKE 16:10 NLT

When my son Joseph was a junior in high school, he felt led to attend the "See You at the Pole" event for the first time. It was his heart's desire to join fellow Christian students and teachers who gathered around their school flagpole to pray and praise the Lord. But when the actual morning arrived, Joseph was having second thoughts about attending because he was so gripped by fear that he felt sick to his stomach. After we sought God in prayer, Joseph "set his face like flint" and took his place next to all the other believers gathered at his school in the Lord's name. My son met a lot of wonderful new Christian friends that day, and they discussed the possibility of starting a Bible club and holding weekly meetings on campus for Bible study and prayer. The Lord gave me a burden to pray for this club to become a reality, even though there had never been a successful one in the history of the school. Weeks turned into months without any sign of a club forming, but I persevered in prayer. Then Joseph shared with me how he felt that God was calling him to approach the school authorities about starting weekly meetings. As he began the process of securing permission to launch a Bible club on campus, the Lord opened one door after another and our dream became a reality. Under Joseph's leadership and the subsequent leadership of my younger son, John, this club touched and changed the lives of a multitude of students from our community and many others.

When I was praying for a high school Bible club, it never occurred to me that the Lord would use my own son to start it. Many of the other Christian students had been believers a lot longer than my son, and in many ways he lacked their spiritual maturity. Nevertheless, God chose Joseph and used him in awesome ways for His glory. I have no doubts that Joseph's attendance at the "See You at the Pole" event that day had everything to do with the Lord choosing him to launch and lead the club. I also believe that my faithfulness in prayer for the club was linked to God's choosing my own son to start it. In addition, the Lord blessed me with some of the most exciting and rewarding years of my life by making me the "Club Mom." As my family and I have walked with God over the years, He has taught us how one small act of obedience on our part can lead to major blessings. Many people are waiting for a "big event" in order to obey God. What they fail to realize is that if they don't obey Him in small matters, their "big event" may never come. Jesus said, "Unless you are faithful in small matters, you won't be

LIVE ON PURPOSE TODAY

Surely as you read these words, little things God is asking of you began to pop into your mind. Make note of them with paper and pen, and then endeavor to demonstrate faithfulness to the Lord by checking off as many as possible before the sun goes down.

faithful in large ones" (Luke 16:10 NLT). Make no mistake—before the Lord will use us to make a difference in this world, we will be tested. We will have to prove to God that He can count on us to obey Him in seemingly insignificant matters, simply because He's the One doing the talking. The truth is that no job that He assigns us is insignificant in His sight. When the Lord leads us "just" to pray for someone or about something, we are partnering with Him just as much as when we're performing a task that brings us considerable recognition. You can bet that when God gives us a seemingly small matter to attend to, Satan will try to convince us that how we respond won't make any difference. He will try to get us to take our obedience casually. This is just one of the many tactics the enemy uses to try to keep us from fulfilling our God-given purpose. I encourage you to begin praying today that the Lord will make you sensitive and obedient to His voice, even in the smallest of matters. Rest assured that heartfelt prayers like these will open the door for God to fill your life with more purpose and meaning than you ever dreamed possible!

PRAYER

Lord, give me a new awareness of how important it is for me to obey You even in the smallest of matters. Make me sensitive and obedient to Your voice, and give me discernment to recognize the voice of the enemy. Don't let me miss out on Your perfect plans for my life. Thank You for making me faithful in little things so that I can be faithful also in much!

A Prophet Without Honor

> *Then Jesus told them, "A prophet is honored everywhere except in his own hometown and among his relatives and his own family."*
>
> MARK 6:4 NLT

This verse has encouraged my heart many times when I've been hurt by the way my loved ones reacted to my commitment to God. The Bible reveals that some of Jesus' friends and family were not the least bit impressed with His ministry or His accomplishments. In fact, Scripture reveals that His own family thought He was "out of his mind" (Mark 3:21). Jesus was misunderstood because of His devotion to the Father and His dedication to the work His Father assigned Him. Why should we be surprised when our loved ones don't understand our commitment to God? The apostle Paul was often misunderstood, too. In 2 Corinthians 5:13, he says, "If we are out of our mind, it is for the sake of God." Seems to me that if people think we have lost our minds because of our love for God, we're in good company.

The truth is that when we decide to live for God, people are not always going to understand or respect us for it. Paul explains why: "The man without the Spirit does not accept the things that come from the Spirit of God, for they are foolishness to him, and he cannot understand them, because they are spiritually discerned" (1 Cor. 2:14). Now that we have the Holy Spirit living in us, we are able to see things from God's perspective. The way we view things will often be radically different than the way others do, and because of that, our priorities will be different. Have you ever accomplished something wonderful for God, and then been met with indifference and disinterest from your friends and loved ones? I have. It can turn our joy into hurt and frustration pretty quickly. Some time ago I gained some media attention

LIVE ON PURPOSE TODAY

Jesus said He would never leave you or forsake you. Take this to heart and thank Him that He is by your side.

because of my work for the Lord. Some of my friends and family were not the least bit impressed. What bothered me most was knowing that if I had been in the public eye because of a sports-related achievement, or because I wrote romance novels, they would have been thrilled. But because I was being recognized for my service to God, they held no esteem for my accomplishments. That was a painful realization for me. Since then I've decided to serve the Lord with all my heart, even if no one else cares. Paul's words in Philippians 3:13-14 have been a great inspiration to me: "But one thing I do: forgetting what lies behind and reaching forward to what lies ahead, I press on toward the goal for the prize of the upward call of God in Christ Jesus." I'm going on with God. How about you?

PRAYER

Lord, thank You for the opportunities You've given me to serve You. Help me to remember that when others don't respect or honor my service to You, it doesn't diminish its value or usefulness in Your sight. Today I renew my wholehearted commitment to You, and I ask You to use me in new and exciting ways for Your glory!

Don't Get Lazy

{ *Don't drag your feet. Be like those who stay the course with committed faith and then get everything promised to them.* }

Recently, some of the problems my family and I had experienced in our neighborhood in the past arose once again. When they first resurfaced, I felt somewhat confused and bewildered. I had prayed and stood on God's promises for peace for my "borders" (Ps. 147:14), and I had witnessed the delivering power of God in mighty ways. But I had begun to take God's blessings for granted. When the problems threatened once again, I sought the Lord for the reason. He promptly pointed out to me that my prayers in that area had gone from earnest to anemic. And He reminded me that I needed to continue to stand in faith for the peace of my neighborhood if I wanted to regain and maintain the victory I had won before.

Hebrews 6:12 says, "We do not want you to become lazy, but to imitate those who through faith and patience inherit what has been promised." I realized that I had become a "spiritual sluggard"—as the Amplified version of this verse says—at least where this issue was concerned. When the problem was at its worst, I used my faith and patience to lay hold of God's promises for the situation. But as soon as the problem showed signs of subsiding, I slacked off. That was a big mistake. Even so, it was a reminder of how important it is for us to continue to stand in faith for God's blessings, even when it looks like our prayers have already been answered. Proverbs 13:4 says, "The sluggard craves and gets nothing, but the desires of the diligent are fully satisfied." Those of us who want God's blessings badly enough to diligently pray for them will find that diligence produces results. Do you ever feel like you want to take a "spiritual vacation"? I

LIVE ON PURPOSE TODAY

Don't make the devil's job easy today! Instead, ask yourself if there are areas in your life in which you've spiritually "slacked off"! Armed with that information, stand on the promises of God and pray with new vigor.

do. There are days when I wake up and think, *I don't feel like praying or standing on God's promises today. I don't feel like reading my Bible or seeking God's face.* But I have found that spiritual passivity can be very costly. Are there areas in your life in which you've spiritually "slacked off"? If so, you may be hindering the flow of God's blessings into your life. Don't make the devil's job easy for him. Satan is relentless, and we need to be relentless, too. Talk to the Lord about any areas in your life that you might be neglecting spiritually, and ask Him to help you get back on track. It won't be long before you're reaping a harvest of blessings that keeps on coming!

PRAYER

Lord, forgive me for the times that I've been a "spiritual sluggard." Give me the grace I need to stand in faith for all of the blessings You have in store for me and my loved ones. When I'm tempted to take a "spiritual vacation," remind me of what it can cost me. Thank You that my diligence will defeat the enemy and glorify You!

The Humble Get the Help

*As the Scriptures say, 'God sets himself against
the proud, but He shows favor to the humble.'*

JAMES 4:6 NLT

Recently, my husband, Joe, taught us all a wonderful lesson in humility. He was driving home from work one evening and was tired and anxious to get home. He knew better than to drive too fast, but he threw caution aside and leaned on the accelerator. As soon as he saw the flashing lights of a police car coming up behind him, he immediately turned to the Lord and humbly asked for His forgiveness and help. When the police officer approached Joe and chastised him for driving so recklessly, my husband admitted his wrongdoing and guilt without hesitation. As a result, the officer did not slap Joe with the severe penalty he deserved, but gave him instead a minor fine and sent him on his way. Overjoyed and grateful, my husband thanked the officer and gave praise to God, vowing to be more careful in the future.

This experience is a perfect example of the truth of James 4:6 NLT which says, "God sets Himself against the proud, but He shows favor to the humble." Time and time again, my family and I have witnessed the difference it makes in our lives and circumstances when we've resisted being prideful and stubborn, and have chosen to humble ourselves before God and others. I can remember a time when my husband would be in exactly the same situation as I just described, but instead of reacting with humility, he would react with anger and stubborn pride. Needless to say, the results were always negative, and sometimes the consequences were even devastating. Once my husband began resisting the temptation to become hostile or offended in situations like these, he began experiencing for himself the goodness of God. Now he's "hooked" and knows that when he's in a "tight spot," the best thing for him to do is to humbly admit his fault and pray for the Lord's forgiveness and help. Why don't more people experience for themselves the goodness of God? The answer is simple—pride. While the Lord earnestly desires to reveal His goodness to us, He can't do that as long as pride is controlling our lives. That's why Satan works overtime trying to get us to become offended, angry, and willful. He knows that these attitudes will drive a wedge between us and God. They will keep us from enjoying the fullness of God's blessings and ultimately prevent us from fulfilling our God-given purpose.

Suppose when that police officer pulled my husband over that day he thought to himself, *I was wrong and I don't deserve the Lord's help, so I won't expect it or ask for it.* This is another mistake that so many of us make. We get caught doing wrong and we decide for ourselves that we don't deserve God's mercy or assistance, so we don't ask for them.

LIVE ON PURPOSE TODAY

Humble yourself and ask God to help you in an area that you have never asked Him to help you before. No matter how confident you may be about your ability in that area, ask Him to help you. Watch what a difference He can make.

This is just as wrong as reacting with anger or hostility. First Peter 5:6-7 TLB says, "If you will humble yourselves under the mighty hand of God, in His good time He will lift you up. Let Him have all your worries and cares, for He is always thinking about you and watching everything that concerns you." The Lord longs to have us humbly turn to Him in our times of need so that He can demonstrate His unconditional love for us and His willingness to act on our behalf. When we make a mistake, God isn't going to make us feel worse by beating us over the head with guilt and condemnation. That's the devil's job. Today, my heartfelt prayer for you is that the next time you're in a "tight spot," you'll remember that it's the humble that get God's help!

PRAYER

Lord, forgive me for the times I've been prideful, angry, or willful. From now on when I'm in trouble, remind me to humbly seek Your help and forgiveness. Give me the grace I need to mature in Christ, and help me to do my part. Thank You for revealing Your goodness and love in awesome new ways!

Ignoring Words of Doubt

> *"…Messengers arrived from Jairus's home with the message,*
> *'Your daughter's dead. There's no use in troubling*
> *the Teacher now.' But Jesus ignored their comments*
> *and said to Jairus, 'Don't be afraid. Just trust me.'"*
>
> MARK 5:35,36 NLT

These verses are some of my favorites in all of Scripture. God has used them many times to encourage my heart when I was in a trial. Not long ago my husband lost his job of 18 years. We knew a year ahead of time that his company would close its doors, and all that time we prayed and stood on God's promises for His provision. Even so, the day came when my husband's job ended, and he still had no idea what he would do. We watched as many unbelievers who never gave the Lord a second thought got wonderful new jobs right away. There were times we were puzzled, hurt, and disappointed. We continued to pray and seek God for His help, and several more months passed by before the Lord opened a door of opportunity for my husband. One thing I discovered during those long and difficult months was that even well-meaning people can say hurtful and negative things. That's when God began teaching me to ignore a lot of the comments others make about certain situations in my life and the lives of my loved ones.

In the above verses, Jairus had appealed to Jesus to come and heal his daughter, who was seriously ill. Before they arrived at Jairus's house, they were told that the little girl had already died.

LIVE ON PURPOSE TODAY

You may not be able to control what people say to you, but you can control how you react. If a negative thought has taken root in your mind, replace it with a verse from God's Word. Replay that Scripture in your mind when that negative thought comes back. You will silence the enemy's plan to discourage you and stop God's best in your life.

Scripture reveals that the Master ignored their comments and asked Jairus to "just trust Him." Each time we're in a trial, we're going to have to choose between trusting God and believing the "negative reports" of others. During difficult times we can be very vulnerable to the remarks that people make about our circumstances, and if we're not careful, we'll take their negative words to heart and become fearful and depressed. If the people around us are not led by God's Spirit, we're not likely to hear God's view of our situation from them. They'll usually give us the world's view, and you can bet it will be one of doom and gloom, especially if it's a particularly serious or "hopeless" situation. They haven't gotten a revelation of how powerful and loving our God is, and how He delights in working wonders for His children who put their faith in Him. And we shouldn't be too surprised if sometimes even fellow believers don't see our situation through God's eyes. Often the Lord will reveal only to us that He has a plan for our deliverance. That's why it's so important for us to ignore others when they make comments filled with doubt and unbelief. We need to turn to God and ask Him to give us *His* view of our situation. Sometimes all we'll hear from Him is "Just trust Me." Sometimes that's all we'll need. The Lord raised Jairus's daughter to life, and He provided my husband with a wonderful new job. If you're in a trial today, let this promise from God encourage your heart: "Trust Me in your times of trouble, and I will rescue you, and you will give Me glory"! (Ps. 50:15 NLT).

PRAYER

Lord, help me to ignore the negative comments of others whenever I go through difficult times. Teach me to listen for Your words of encouragement and hope. Give me the faith to trust You for my deliverance, and guard me from fear and doubt. Thank You for the wonders You'll work in my life as I trust in You!

Saying "No" to Self-Pity

*The bread of idleness (gossip, discontent, and self-pity)
she (the virtuous woman) will not eat.*

PROVERBS 31:27 AMP

I recently went through some difficulties that got me so discouraged that I found myself wrestling with feelings of self-pity. Years ago I might have played some sad songs and cried my eyes out, deriving a sort of perverse satisfaction from my misery. But this time I prayed and asked the Lord to help me resist these negative emotions. That's when He reminded me about some teaching I heard years ago about self-pity. I once heard a godly man say, "God is concerned about your hurt, but He doesn't want *you* concerned about it." This man went on to say that the reason self-pity is so destructive is that pride is at the root of it, and it causes us to focus too much on ourselves. I looked *self-pity* up in the dictionary and found the following definition: "Pity for oneself; especially a self-indulgent dwelling on one's own sorrows or misfortunes."[4]

Psychiatrists have an interesting name for people who habitually indulge in self-pity—it's "injustice collector." These are the folks who are constantly dwelling on their hurts and hardships—whether real or imagined—and they enjoy thinking about them and talking about them. They lovingly collect and number each and every offense that others commit against them, and they search out people who will sympathize with them and commiserate with them. All this keeps the focus on themselves, which is what they want most. But this isn't God's way. He instructs us to walk in the God-kind of love, which is "not self-seeking," and which "keeps no record of wrongs" (1 Cor. 13:5). This is not to say that we should ignore or deny when we're being mistreated, but that we should take constructive action to see that we're treated with proper respect, or to remove ourselves from harm's way, rather than sit idly by, feeling sorry for ourselves. Self-pity isn't just nonproductive—it's destructive. It can lead to bitterness, unforgiveness, and resentment. It doesn't bring people together—it divides them. And these are some of the reasons why Satan works so hard to get us to focus on our wounds, rather than the cure—which is the love and wisdom of God. Throughout the pages of the Bible, God tells us again and again that He wants us to bring our hurts and sorrows to Him so that *He* can comfort us. He not only wants to be our Comforter, but our Vindicator. (Ps. 135:14.) If we'll let Him, He will defend us and fight our battles for us, leading us to victory every time. He tells us in His Word, "I, the Lord, love justice. I hate robbery and wrongdoing. I will faithfully reward my people for their suffering..." (Isa. 61:8 NLT).

LIVE ON PURPOSE TODAY

If you find yourself saying, "poor me," stop. Write down your thoughts of hurt or hardships. Get them out of your mind and give them to God. As a demonstration, throw away the paper you just wrote them on. The pity-party is over!

A good antidote for self-pity is forgiveness. As we forgive those who offend us, we can let go of our negative emotions and ill-feelings toward others, and we can receive the comfort and healing that can only come from God. Scripture says, "In all their suffering He also suffered, and He personally rescued them. In His love and mercy, He redeemed them. He lifted them up and carried them through all the years" (Isa. 63:9 NLT). God hurts when we hurt, and He wants to be our Deliverer. But we can block His efforts to comfort and rescue us when we insist on holding on to our feelings of resentment, bitterness, and unforgiveness. As we choose to forgive, we open the door to God's involvement, and all the blessings and provisions that entails. Another good antidote for self-pity is thankfulness. The Bible says, "Thank [God] in everything [no matter what the circumstances may be, be thankful and give thanks], for this is the will of God for you [who are] in Christ Jesus" (1 Thess. 5:18 AMP). No matter what is going on in our lives, we always have reason to give thanks to God and praise Him. Nothing is more offensive to God than our dwelling on our misfortunes and losses, and neglecting to recognize and enumerate all of the blessings He bestows on us daily.

Helen Keller said, "Self-pity is our worst enemy and if we yield to it, we can never do anything good in the world." We have been chosen by God, not just to live eternally with Him in heaven, but to make a difference for Him while we're still here on earth. Let's not allow self-pity to neutralize all the good we can do in this world in the name of Jesus.

PRAYER

Lord, please alert me whenever I begin to feel sorry for myself. Keep me from being overly-sensitive and self-absorbed, and teach me to bring all of my hurts and hardships straight to You. When I do, heal and comfort me the way that only You can. Give me the grace I need to forgive others quickly and thoroughly, and to praise You in all things. Thank You that as I resist self-pity in the power of Your Spirit, I will be rewarded by a gracious and grateful God!

Keeping Our Dreams in Proper Perspective

Each one should use whatever gift he has received to serve others,
faithfully administering God's grace in its various forms.
If anyone serves, he should do it with the strength God provides,
so that in all things God may be praised through Jesus Christ.

1 PETER 4:10,11

Several years ago I saw a famous Christian singer being interviewed on television. She was talking about how she had always wanted to reach millions for Christ with her musical talents and to glorify God with her popularity. Then she said something that really made an impression on me and that has stuck with me till this day. She said that she decided long ago that if the Lord didn't allow her dream to be fulfilled, she would just depend on Him to give her the grace to deal with it—and she would go on and enjoy her life just the same. What I admired most about this young woman was that she had the faith and the courage to put her dreams and desires "on the altar," and to leave them in God's hands. She admitted that she would have been sorely disappointed if her dreams didn't come to pass, but she refused to have a "do or die" attitude about her heartfelt desires, and she surrendered them to the Lord.

There's nothing wrong with having visions, dreams, and goals. God wants us to have these things. But He wants us to have goals that line up with His will for us. When we get into agreement with God's will and purposes for our lives, there's no devil in hell, no person on earth, that can stop them from coming to pass. In fact, the only one who can really stand between us and our God-given destiny is us. Satan can't. Our families can't. Our bosses can't. Even the government can't. No one can prevent us from becoming the person of God that we were created to be. Except us. We can live our lives the way we want to, and we can turn our backs on God's perfect plans for us, if we so choose. And in the end, all we will have to show for it is regret. Or we can get in line with God's will for us, and we can watch Him unfold our lives like a beautiful flower, one petal at a time. We can do this by surrendering ourselves to the Lord—spirit, soul, and body—and by seeking Him and His will for us every day of our lives through prayer, devotion, and the study of His Word.

One thing I've learned from walking with the Lord these ten years is this: God will test our devotion to Him by letting us experience times of disappointment, especially where the fulfillment of our dreams is concerned. How we respond to these disappointments will help determine how much God can use us and bless us. If we respond with pouting, sulking, complaining, or threatening, God will have to treat us like the babies we're imitating, and He will not be able to trust us with the level of responsibility or blessing He longs to. But if we respond with an attitude that says—"God, I don't understand this, and it really hurts, but I believe that You are good, and You will work this out for my good"—the Lord will reward our faithfulness and spiritual maturity beyond our highest expectations. I recently heard a definition for *idol* that made me shudder. It said, "An idol is anything you feel you can't live without and be happy." It can be a dream, a desire, a thing, or even a person. The Bible says that our God is a jealous God, and He's not about to share us with anything or anyone else. (Ex. 20:5.) He expects our wholehearted devotion, and He deserves it, simply because He's God. If we ever find ourselves desiring something so much that we feel we can't live without it, God may close the door to it—either temporarily or permanently—depending on what He feels is best for our spiritual well-being.

LIVE ON PURPOSE TODAY

Refocus your dreams. Take five minutes and write down what you would like to accomplish in the future. Pray and commit these desires to God in light of His will for your life.

The Lord wants us to be able to say with all sincerity, "God, I can live without this dream—but I can't live without *You!*" With an attitude like this, we can walk in the awesome plans and purposes that God has mapped out for us, and we can have all the joy, peace, and fulfillment that are ours in Christ.

If God has closed a door on a heartfelt desire or dream of yours today, take comfort in the fact that He is saying to you one of two things. Either it's, "Wait. It's not the right time yet." Or, "I have something better for you." In either case, you can't lose, because you have put your trust in a God who loves you with a perfect love and who has your best interests at heart!

PRAYER

Lord, show me Your will and purposes for my life, and help me to make them my personal goals. Help me to always give You first place in my life so that everything else will fall into place. When I experience disappointment and heartache, comfort me and fill me with a fresh sense of hope. I can live without the things of this world, Lord—but I can't live without You!

Good Reason To Hope

We have this hope as an anchor for the soul, firm and secure.

HEBREWS 6:19

The last time I went through a dark and difficult period in my life, the Lord showed me this verse and gave me new and valuable insight through it. He showed me how I could remain more stable during trials and tribulations if I would purposefully place my hope in Him and His Word, allowing that hope to act as an anchor for my soul. As He reminded me that our soul is made up of our mind, will, and emotions, I began to understand how learning the principles in this verse could make me more stable and help me avoid being tossed to and fro by the people and circumstances surrounding me.

We could all benefit from using some positive self-talk the way the psalmist often did. Psalm 43:5 says, "Why are you downcast, O my soul? Why so disturbed within me? Put your hope in God, for I will yet praise him, my Savior and my God." The author is talking to the soulish part of himself here, saying that by placing his hope firmly in God he will find relief from discouragement and despair. In Psalm 27:13 NASB, David writes, "I would have despaired unless I had believed that I would see the goodness of the Lord in the land of the living." Notice that David didn't have to actually see God's goodness before he found relief from despair; he only had to *believe* he would see it, and that was enough. Perhaps when you're going through difficult times, you find it hard to believe. I can relate to that. But recently, God led me to some wonderful insights from a godly man who said that if we think of faith as a *choice* rather than an *ability*, we will understand that faith is actually simpler than it seems. And we can ask the Lord to help us to make that choice. Psalm 31:24 NKJV says, "Be of good courage, and He shall strengthen your heart, all you who hope in the Lord." As we do our part by making the decision to take our stand in faith and to place our hope in God, He has promised to do His part by strengthening us and helping us stand firm till the victory comes.

Look at the role that hope plays in the psalmist's prayer in Psalm 33:22: "May Your unfailing love rest upon us, O Lord, even as we put our hope in You." The author is saying here, "Bless us to the same degree that we put our hope in You, Lord." The Amplified translation says it best: "Let Your mercy and loving-kindness, O Lord, be upon us in proportion to our waiting and hoping for You." The Bible makes it clear that God is pleased when we place our hope in Him and His goodness, and He is eager to reward us when we do. Psalm 33:18-19 says, "The eyes of the Lord are on those who fear Him, on those whose hope is in His unfailing love, to deliver them from death

LIVE ON PURPOSE TODAY

Without hope we cannot have faith. Our faith is the evidence of what we are hoping for. Write down one thing that you hope for. Write next to it a Scripture promise that you can put your faith on and connect your faith to your hope. Thank God that the victory is yours.

and keep them alive in famine." This is God's promise of protection and provision to those who choose to put their trust in Him in times of adversity. As long as I can remember, I have always believed in God. But it wasn't until I began devoting myself to His Word that I had something tangible that I could hang on to when times got rough. I can easily relate to the psalmist's sentiment when he says, "Your Word is my only source of hope" (Ps. 119:114 NLT). There have been many times when my faith was stretched to the limit, and all I could do was cling to God's promise in Isaiah 49:23: "Those who hope in Me will not be disappointed." I can't promise that every time you place your hope in God things will turn out exactly the way you want them to. But I *can* promise you that every time you choose to hope instead of doubt, the Lord will honor your faith somehow. And that is why I urge you today—"Wait for God. Wait with hope. Hope now; hope always!" (Ps. 131:3 MESSAGE).

PRAYER

Lord, teach me how to be more stable in difficult times. Reveal to me how putting my hope in You, Your Word, and Your goodness will open the door for me to receive all the blessings You have in store for me. Remind me how maintaining a hopeful attitude can be the best antidote for discouragement and despair. Thank You that as I do my part in gaining the victory, You will do Yours!

The Moment We Pray

{ *The moment you began praying, a command was given...for God loves you very much.* }

DANIEL 9:23 NLT

My sister and her husband have owned a car repair business for many years. A few months ago they began to have some serious problems with one of the business owners in their neighborhood. This man began allowing his son to manage his business affairs, and this son quickly became a thorn in my sister's, and her husband's, side. A disagreement broke out about parking spaces the two businesses had formerly shared, and what began as a minor altercation became a major battle. My sister became anxious and depressed, and she called on me for prayer and words of encouragement. I assured her that her problem was not too big for God to handle, and we began to stand in faith for His intervention. We prayed for godly wisdom and guidance, and we asked the Lord to show us what my sister's part was in bringing a speedy resolution to the problem. A few weeks later she called me to say that she had ordered new parking signs to clearly establish boundaries between her own property lines and her neighbor's. She told me that the very day these signs arrived, she discovered that the business next door had been sold. We thanked and praised God because, not only had He delivered her from her disagreeable neighbor, but He had directed her steps so that her boundaries were clearly marked in advance of the new neighbor's arrival.

My sister's experience reminded me of some words spoken by an angel of God to the prophet Daniel after he had begun earnestly praying for his nation's deliverance. Daniel was told, "The moment you began praying, a command was given...for God loves you very much" (Dan. 9:23 NLT). When my sister first began praying for the Lord's help, she didn't see any signs to indicate that He had even heard her prayers. For a long time she had to trust that God did indeed hear her pleas and that He was busy working behind the scenes to bring her deliverance to pass. It wasn't until that day she received her new parking signs, and discovered that she would have new business neighbors, that she knew with certainty that the Lord had been working on her behalf all along.

I was greatly encouraged by my sister's experience, and you should be, too. It's a reminder of how our God begins working behind the scenes on our behalf as soon as we call on Him for help. King David knew this, and that's why He wrote, "The very day I call for help, the tide of battle turns. My enemies flee! This one thing I know: God is for me!" (Ps. 56:9 TLB). Just because we don't see any clear signs that the Lord is working on our problems, that doesn't mean that He's

LIVE ON PURPOSE TODAY

With God everything can change in a moment. Maybe you have been waiting for that moment of change for a while. Don't give up—God is working on your behalf. Remember a time when God came through for you at just the right moment— not a moment too soon or a moment too late. Commit to trust Him today.

not doing exactly that. God does most of His work behind the scenes, and if we will remember that, we will be less tempted to lose heart and quit standing in faith for our victory before it comes to pass. The Book of Daniel reveals that sometimes the answers to our prayers are delayed because of resistance from evil forces in the spiritual realm. The angel that appeared to Daniel told him, "Don't be afraid, Daniel. Since the first day you began to pray for understanding and to humble yourself before God, your request has been heard in heaven. I have come in answer to your prayer. But for twenty-one days, the spirit prince of the kingdom of Persia blocked my way. Then Michael, one of the archangels, came to help me..." (Dan. 10:12,13 NLT). Satan and his cohorts are formidable enemies, but they're no match for God. As we pray and stand in faith for His help, God will move heaven and earth to see that we receive the victories He has in store for us. Today, rest assured that as long as you are seeking God's help and trusting Him to come to your aid, He is busy working behind the scenes on your behalf. So hang in there, beloved, because help is on the way!

PRAYER

Lord, help me to always turn to You first when troubles arise. Teach me how to pray and stand in faith for the victories You don't want me to miss out on. Remind me that even when I don't see any tangible signs of Your involvement, You began working on my behalf the moment I began reaching out to You in prayer. Thank You, Lord, that even though my blessings may be delayed, they are guaranteed by You!

The Power of God's Word

The Word of God is full of living power.
It is sharper than the sharpest knife, cutting
deep into our innermost thoughts and desires.

HEBREWS 4:12 NLT

I once read a true story about how a minister spoke God's Word over a friend in the hospital, and witnessed its powerful effect on the patient's heart monitor, as well as on the patient herself. Here was modern technology recording and confirming the inherent power in God's Holy Word.

I'm convinced that if believers had a real awareness of just how powerful God's Word is, they would pay more attention to it. When Joshua was taking over Moses' job, God told him to meditate on His Word day and night. The Lord told Joshua that this was how he would be able to perform the will of God and be prosperous and successful. (Josh. 1:8.) And in Proverbs 4:20-22, the Lord says that His Word is life and health to those who pay attention to it. If you're willing to invest some time and energy reading, memorizing, and meditating on the Word of God, you can experience dramatic, positive changes in every area of your life. Let me share with you some simple but powerful principles that the Lord has shown me in recent years.

We can honor God by quoting and meditating on His Word three ways: (1) by putting a verse in prayer form, (2) by making it a declaration of faith, and (3) by turning it into an expression of praise. For example, each day I pray, "Lord, order my steps this day," which is based on Psalm 37:23 KJV. Then throughout the day

I reaffirm God's answer to my prayer for guidance by declaring, "My steps are ordered by the Lord!" If doubt and fear begin to assail me, I encourage myself by praising Him for the answer with, "Thank You, Lord, that my steps are ordered by You!" If I have a need, I claim Philippians 4:19 and quote it according to my specific need. "Thank You, Lord, that You supply all my job needs!" I have used this verse to seek God for every conceivable need, including financial, healing, material, and social needs. I combine my faith with my declarations, according to Hebrews 4:2, and as a result, rest and peace flood my mind and heart. God's Word has the ability to build our faith, renew our minds, and change our hearts. If we don't meditate on God's truths day and night, we will be easy targets for Satan's deceptions. Declaring God's Word is not mind over matter—it's truth over error. Jesus used Scripture to defeat Satan when he came to tempt the Savior in the wilderness, and we can do the same thing. (Luke 4:1-12.) Each day of our lives we have two choices—we can meditate on God's promises, or we can meditate on our problems. Meditating on God's Word can bring peace, joy, life, and health. Meditating on our problems can cause anxiety, fear, despair, and sickness. The Bible tells us to "be imitators of God" (Eph. 5:1). Do you think God is wringing His hands, wondering what He's going to do about our problems? No way. The Bible says He's "watching over His Word to perform and fulfill it" on our behalf (Jer. 1:12). So let's give Him something to work with. Let's honor

LIVE ON PURPOSE TODAY

Declare God's Word as truth over error in your life today, and honor God by quoting and meditating on His Word in the three ways shared: Put a verse in prayer form, make it a declaration of faith, and turn it into an expression of praise.

our God by letting Him hear His precious Word on our lips day and night, for only then will we be prosperous and successful for His glory!

PRAYER

Lord, fill my heart with a growing passion for Your Word. Help me to believe, declare, and act upon it for my good and Your glory. Show me how to apply Your truth to every area of my life. Thank You, Lord, that Your Word is true and You are true to Your Word! (John 17:17; Heb. 11:11 AMP.)

When Trouble Strikes

I will call to You whenever trouble strikes, and You will help me.

PSALM 86:7 TLB

For most of my life I had a mindset that almost expected trouble. I was raised as a Christian, and I was brought up hearing the Savior's words—"In this world, you will have trouble" (John 16:33). So it seemed natural to me that I should expect—and even count on—having problems throughout my life. As a result, when adversity struck me or my loved ones, my prayers for help were often timid and halfhearted. It wasn't until I was married and had teenaged children that I got serious about my relationship with God and began studying His Word. I was delighted to discover that the Bible was filled with godly men and women who boldly called upon the Lord in their times of trouble and were often delivered in miraculous ways.

One such person was King David. When we study David's life and writings, we discover that when this man of God encountered trouble, he was quick to call upon his divine Deliverer. David didn't just pray for relief or help—he prayed for victory. He didn't hesitate to pour out his heart to God, or to let the Lord know exactly what he was feeling. And he was humble enough to admit his need for God and his dependence upon Him. David wrote, "In the day of my trouble I will call to You, for You will answer me" (Ps. 86:7). I believe that this attitude of David's was one of the secrets of his enormous success.

Psalm 34 is one of the most quoted and beloved psalms in the Bible. In it, David mentions the delivering power of God three times. He says, "A righteous man may have many troubles, but the Lord delivers him from them all" (v. 19). David is not in denial. He freely admits that God's people are not exempt from problems. But he chooses to focus on God's ability and willingness to save and deliver. In verses 6 and 17 of this psalm, David reveals that God's entire rescue operation is put into action as a result of prayer. He writes, "The righteous cry out, and the Lord hears them; He delivers them from all their troubles" (Ps. 34:17).

It's true that Jesus said, "In this world, you will have trouble." But it's also true that He went on to say, "But take heart! I have overcome the world" (John 16:33). The Savior was not trying to discourage us with these words. He was trying to encourage our hearts and give us hope. He was telling us that even though we'll go through some hard times, they won't be able to defeat us, if we'll live our daily lives trusting in Him and depending on Him for guidance and strength. And even though there will be problems in our lives that are simply unavoidable no matter what we do, there will be some that we can escape by making right choices. Proverbs 19:23 says, "The fear of the Lord leads to life: Then one rests content, untouched by trouble." This is God's assurance that by trusting and obeying Him, we can minimize the amount of trouble that we'll encounter in our daily lives. The psalmist wrote, "Blessed is the man You

LIVE ON PURPOSE TODAY

What is troubling you today? Find a Scripture that you can stand on. When the devil tries to get you down, repeat that Scripture to him. God is our Deliverer!

discipline, O Lord, the man You teach from Your law; You grant him relief from trouble, till a pit is dug for the wicked" (Ps. 95:12,13). Those believers who devote themselves to the Word of God—studying it and doing it—will be able to avoid many of the pitfalls that the enemy puts in their path. I know from experience that ignorance of God's Word can be costly and painful. Prayerlessness can be costly, too. We will encounter more trouble than we need to if we fail to pray regularly for protection from it. Jabez prayed, "Keep me from all trouble and pain!" (1 Chron. 4:10 NLT). We know that God was pleased with his prayer because Scripture says, "And God granted his request."

James wrote, "Is any one of you in trouble? He should pray" (James 5:13). Notice that he didn't say we should whine, complain, or get angry. He didn't say we should just accept our lot and be grateful that things aren't any worse. He said we should *pray*. This is a common theme throughout the Bible, and it's one we should take seriously and apply to our own lives. It's my heartfelt prayer that this precious invitation and promise from God would inspire and challenge you today: "Call upon Me in the day of trouble; I will deliver you and you will honor Me" (Ps. 50:15).

PRAYER

Lord, when trouble strikes, teach me to pray for deliverance with confidence and boldness. Help me to devote myself to You and Your Word so that I can avoid as many problems as possible. Thank You, Lord, that You will be with me in trouble as I call upon You; You will deliver me and honor Me, according to Your Word! (Ps. 91:15).

Even Now

But I know that even now God will give you whatever you ask.

JOHN 11:22

These words were spoken to Jesus by Martha, the sister of Lazarus. Her brother had already been dead four days by the time Jesus arrived. Yet here she confesses her faith in the Savior to do even the impossible. Moments later Martha witnesses a miracle as her brother is raised to life by the Master.

A few years ago God began bringing me up to a new level of faith. He taught me how to pray what I now refer to as my "even now" prayers. I would be facing an impossible situation, and it would seem like all the doors before me had been closed. My first impression would be to think, *I guess it just wasn't God's will.* Then I would sense another impression coming up in my spirit telling me to continue praying in faith. I might pray something like this: "Lord, I admit this looks like a hopeless situation, but I know that even now, You can make a way where there seems to be none. I ask that You do that, Lord." I have seen so many seemingly closed doors opened by praying like this, that my prayer life has been radically changed forever. And I have used this principle in praying about small matters, as well as big ones.

Jesus said, "The things which are impossible with men are possible with God" (Luke 18:27 NKJV). I think it's sad that our society has gotten so sophisticated and cynical that we've forgotten how to pray for the impossible. In Jeremiah 32:27, the Lord says, "I am the Lord, the God of all mankind. Is anything too hard for me?" This statement should not only encourage us, but it should convict us as well. Psalm 77:19 TLB says, "Your road led by a pathway through the sea— a pathway no one knew was there!" The Israelites never could have imagined that God would make a way for them through the Red Sea. Likewise, when we pray for the impossible, God will often make a way for us that will exceed our expectations. Psalm 77:14 TLB says, "You are the God of miracles and wonders! You still demonstrate your awesome power." When

LIVE ON PURPOSE TODAY

Do you feel like you are facing the Red Sea? Set your faith on what seems impossible and don't look back. Write down exactly what you are believing God to do and today's date next to it. Commit it to God. Hang on to what you have written. You will be able to look back and have a documented record of His extraordinary faithfulness.

we ask God for the impossible, we invite Him to work wonders in our lives—something He delights in doing. Have you given up on a dream or vision that God has planted in your heart, because at this point it looks like it can never come to pass? What "impossible" situations do you have in your life right now that maybe you've given up on too soon? Perhaps the Lord is just waiting for you to come to Him in faith today, saying, "Lord, I know that even now…."

PRAYER

Lord, I ask that You increase my faith and expand my vision so that I can trust You to do the impossible in my life. Help me to never put limits on You. When I'm tempted to give up on a situation too soon, remind me to ask You to make a way where there seems to be none. Thank You that You are the God of the impossible!

Keep on Believing

Do not be seized with alarm and struck with fear;
only keep on believing.

MARK 5:36 AMP

While my son was growing up, he often experienced bothersome foot problems. They never posed a serious threat, and we always seemed able to manage them with home remedies and prayer. But on one occasion when my son was in his teens, he hid his foot ailments from me until they were so severe that we had to seek medical attention. As we waited a week to get an appointment with our doctor, we prayed and stood on God's Word, trusting Him to spare my son from surgery of any kind. But upon examination, the doctor determined that surgery was unavoidable, and it was performed that very day. I must admit that afterwards I felt defeated and disappointed. I really believed that God would intervene on my son's behalf, and I felt let down when He didn't. Later that evening a friend came by to visit. She began telling me how two of her family members had the same surgery and experienced excruciating pain afterwards. As I listened to her unsettling reports, fear gripped me from head to toe. Then suddenly I sensed a Holy Spirit resistance rising up inside of me. And even though I felt like my faith had been badly shaken earlier that day, I made the decision to ask God to grant my son a pain-free recovery. I got in touch with a friend who I knew I could count on to agree in prayer with me for a miracle. And what began as a deflating experience turned into one of victory and elation. The pain-free recovery the Lord granted my son that day has inspired us to pray for extraordinary recoveries for others, as well.

This experience made me realize that there are times when we are too quick to throw away our faith when we're faced with disappointment because our prayers aren't answered as we expected. Hebrews 10:35 NLT says, "Do not throw away this confident trust in the Lord, no matter what happens. Remember the great reward it brings you!" It would have been very easy for me to remain doubtful and discouraged after my son underwent the surgery I had prayed against. But because I determined to shake off my doubts and reach out for a miracle in the face of apparent defeat, God honored my faith by working wonders for my son. In chapter 5 of the Gospel of Mark, a man named Jairus asks Jesus to come heal his dying daughter. Before they reach the man's home, they are met with the news that the girl is already dead. The Master turns to Jairus and says, "Do not be seized with alarm and struck with fear; only keep on believing" (Mark 5:36 AMP). This account is a message of hope and encouragement to those of us who have trusted the Lord for help but have been met with disappointment and defeat. When the Lord tells us to "keep on believing," He's basically

LIVE ON PURPOSE TODAY

Take a step back from your current situation. Even though it is easy to focus on disappointment, take comfort in what God's Word says about it. List one Scripture that expresses God's thoughts about what you are going through and carry it around in your wallet or pocket to encourage you today.

saying, "I know things look bad right now, but don't lose your faith in Me. Give Me the opportunity to reveal My presence and power in the midst of this apparent defeat." I believe that these "apparent defeats" are some of the greatest opportunities we will ever have to witness the miracle-working power of God in our lives. What circumstances are in your life right now that the Lord might want you to apply this message to? Ask Him today, promising Him your willingness to trust Him even in the hopeless situations He doesn't want you to give up on. May our declaration of faith always be: "But as for me, I will always have hope; I will praise You more and more"! (Ps. 71:14).

PRAYER

Lord, give me the wisdom and discernment I need to know when it's Your will for me to "keep on believing" in the face of apparent defeat. Teach me how to open the door for You to work wonders in my life. Thank You that my confident trust in You will be richly rewarded!

Overlooked and Unappreciated

> *Then the king said to Zadok, "Take the ark of God back into*
> *the city. If I find favor in the Lord's eyes, He will bring me*
> *back and let me see it and His dwelling place again. But if*
> *He says, 'I am not pleased with you,' then I am ready;*
> *let Him do to me whatever seems good to Him."*
>
> 2 SAMUEL 15:25,26

These words of King David have been a profound inspiration to me at times when I've felt overlooked, passed over, or treated unfairly. David is considered by many to be the most victorious warrior of all time, and yet when his own son, Absalom, conspires against him to steal his throne, instead of retaliating, he commits himself to God and His sense of justice. He doesn't whine, complain, or feel sorry for himself. He just basically says, "Lord, I put myself in Your hands. Do with me whatever You think is right. I trust You." And David's attitude was a Christlike one, according to the Scripture which says, "When [Jesus] suffered, He did not threaten to get even. He left His case in the hands of God, who always judges fairly" (1 Peter 2:23 NLT). As it turned out, the Lord did restore David to his throne, and I believe that his unwavering trust in God was the main reason why.

Sooner or later all of us will experience the pain and disappointment of having our efforts ignored, minimized, or criticized by others. I believe that how we respond in times like these not only indicates our level of spiritual maturity, but also determines our outcome. One thing that helps me is remembering that what-ever we do should be done "unto the Lord." The apostle Paul wrote, "Work hard and cheerfully at all you do, just as though you were working for the Lord and not merely for your masters, remembering that it is the Lord Christ who is going to pay you, giving you your full portion of all He owns. He is the one you are really working for" (Col. 3:23,24 TLB). These verses clearly convey the perspective we should have in all we do. If we focus on pleas-ing God and doing our best in everything, we won't be so resent-ful, hurt, or discouraged when others don't appreciate or reward our efforts. Instead, we can rest secure in the knowledge that God is fully aware of all we do, and He will see that we get the recognition and reward we deserve in His perfect way and timing. Even if those we are working for are continu-ally unreasonable or unfair, we can take heart from God's reassurance that "nothing can hinder the Lord" (1 Sam. 14:6 NLT). There may be times when it looks like others are succeeding in delaying or preventing our progress, but the truth is that when God decides to bless and promote His people, no person on earth and no devil in hell can stop Him. If you can relate to this message today, let me encourage you to get your eyes off other people and get them squarely on God. Work hard and do your best in all you do, trusting that the Lord Himself will honor you for it, even if others don't. Let your declaration of faith be the psalmist's—"You will give me greater honor than before, and turn again and comfort me"! (Ps. 71:21 TLB).

LIVE ON PURPOSE TODAY

When you're tempted to feel overlooked and unappreciated, encourage yourself with the Scriptures above. Read them, meditate upon them, and be enlivened by them!

PRAYER

Lord, I believe that true honor and promotion come from You. (Ps. 75:6,7 TLB.) When my efforts are overlooked or unappreciated, I ask that You help me to respond in a Christlike manner. Strengthen me to resist becoming angry, resentful, frustrated, or discouraged. Show me how to pray for those who treat me unfairly. Thank You that as I depend on You for justice and reward, You will lift me up and exalt me at the proper time! (1 Peter 5:6.)

Help in Our Struggles

For God is working in you, giving you the desire to
obey Him and the power to do what pleases Him.

PHILIPPIANS 2:13 NLT

I can still remember the first time I saw this verse in the Bible. I had been struggling in my walk with God, and I had become frustrated and discouraged. I wasn't satisfied with my spiritual progress, and I was disgusted with my many shortcomings. God used this verse to reassure me that I was not alone in my struggles. He showed me that He is always at work in me, giving me the desire and the power to do His will. I still stand on this promise every day, especially when I'm having trouble obeying God, or when the enemy is assailing me with guilt and condemnation. Philippians 1:6 says, "He who began a good work in you will carry it on to completion until the day of Christ Jesus." God has promised that He's not going to abandon us or give up on us; He will stick with us and work with us each and every day of our lives. Psalm 23:3 NKJV says, "He leads me in the paths of righteousness for His name's sake." The Living Bible puts it this way: "He helps me do what honors Him the most." Once we have received Christ as our Savior, God is committed to helping us grow in grace and to become increasingly more Christlike. Philippians 4:13 TLB says, "I can do everything God asks me to with the help of Christ who gives me the strength and the power." God will never ask us to do anything that He won't empower us to do. The enemy will try to convince us otherwise, but we must not make the mistake of falling for his lies.

I love what the apostle Paul says in his letter to the Galatians: "Have you lost your senses? After starting your Christian lives in the Spirit, why are you now trying to become perfect by your own human effort?" (Gal. 3:3 NLT). Paul points out that it's God who saves us and fills us with His Spirit as a result of our believing the message of the Gospel. And it is God who, by the power of His Spirit, helps us grow spiritually. We can't earn our salvation or become Christlike through our own human efforts. All we can do is cooperate with God and allow Him to transform us into the likeness of Christ a little at a time. Sometimes we can feel overwhelmed when we think of how far we are from being like Jesus. We need to remember that God can't deal with us about all our sins at the same time because it would crush us. At just the right time the Holy Spirit will convict us about a particular sin. That's when we need to agree with God that we are sinning. Then we need to ask for God's forgiveness and for His help to do His will. God will show us steps we can take to do our part in the process. As we do our part, God does His by giving us the power to obey Him. Some of our deliverances will come more quickly than others. One of the most powerful prayers we can ever pray is, "Lord, change me." If you'll pray like this every day with all your heart,

LIVE ON PURPOSE TODAY

When facing temptation or discouragement, instead of falling into old patterns of defeat, invite God into the midst of it. Throughout the day, if discouraging or tempting thoughts come, simply say, "Jesus, I invite You into my life in this moment." Discover what a difference that simple prayer can make.

God will do awesome things in and through you. Most of all, always remember that God sees our hearts. He knows we love Him and want to please Him. Let me leave you with a promise from God to encourage your heart today: "Now may the God of peace make you holy in every way, and may your whole spirit and soul and body be kept blameless until that day when our Lord Jesus Christ comes again. God, who calls you, is faithful; *He* will do this"! (1 Thess. 5:23,24 NLT).

PRAYER

Lord, when I feel overwhelmed by my shortcomings, grant
me Your reassurance and sustain me with Your peace.
Give me the desire and the power to do what pleases
You in all things. Show me how to cooperate with Your plan
to make me more like Jesus each day. Thank You for turning
my discouragement and defeat into victory and praise!

Praying God's Will

{ *"This is the confidence we have in approaching God:
that if we ask anything according to his will, he hears us.
And if we know that he hears us—whatever we ask—
we know that we have what we asked of him."* }

1 JOHN 5:14,15

In these verses, the apostle John assures us that we can have
"confidence" in prayer. The key, he says, is praying in line with
God's will. I have found that the best place to start in praying
according to the will of God is with His Word. No matter what we
are facing, God has instructions, insights, and promises that apply
to our situation. The Bible reveals God's will concerning our relationships, health, finances, education, vocation, and everything
else pertaining to our lives here on earth. It's up to us to search
out the verses that relate to our situation and ask the Lord how
we can apply them. Jesus said, "If ye abide in Me, and My words
abide in you, ye shall ask what ye will, and it shall be done unto
you" (John 15:7 KJV). It is in knowing and believing God's Word
that our hearts and minds are transformed, and our wills become
aligned with God's. We are then able to pray the prayers of God's
own heart, and as a result, we are assured of the answer to our
prayers. Romans 12:2 NLT says, "Don't copy the behavior and
customs of this world, but let God transform you into a new
person by changing the way you think. Then you will know what
God wants you to do, and you will know how good and pleasing
and perfect his will really is." In this verse, the apostle Paul urges
us to allow God to renew our minds so that we will be able to

{ 219 }

prove what His perfect will is. We can cooperate with God's plan to transform our thinking by studying, believing, and meditating on His Word. In this way, we will reprogram our minds with God's truth and leave behind the worldly, negative thinking which would cause us to pray ineffectively and with little or no results.

Not only has God given us His Word to help us pray effectively, but He has also given us His Spirit. Romans 8:26 NLT says, "The Holy Spirit helps us in our distress. For we don't even know what we should pray for, nor how we should pray. But the Holy Spirit prays for us." And the next verse tells us that "the Spirit pleads for us believers in harmony with God's own will." God knows there will be times when we won't know how to pray correctly, and He has made special provision for us in those times through His Spirit. We don't have to be at the mercy of our emotions in trying times, but we can call upon God and ask Him to help us pray the prayers of His own heart through His Spirit. The Bible is a source of wonderful Spirit-given prayers we can apply to our lives and situations. As believers, we have the privilege—and often the obligation—to pray the same prayers that Jesus, Paul, and David did for ourselves and others. And no matter what comes our way, we can rest assured

LIVE ON PURPOSE TODAY

The Spirit of God inspired the apostle Paul to pray some mighty prayers—prayers that are also important for you to pray. Open your Bible now to Ephesians 1:15-23, Ephesians 3:13-21, Philippians 1:9-11, and Colossians 1:9-11, and pray these inspired prayers inserting your name. They will bless you abundantly!

that God has promises in His Word that we can pray and stand on for our deliverance and victory. If we go to God with our troubles and concerns and ask Him for a promise of our very own to claim, He will show it to us. Then it's up to us to lay hold of that promise by faith and stand on it until our answer comes. And let's never forget that God sees our hearts. If we have a sincere desire to please Him and we trust that He always wants the best for us, we can pray the way we feel "led" to. Even if we "miss" God, He will redirect us and turn our hearts toward His will, simply because He knows we love Him. It's my prayer that you would begin praying with confidence and discover the joy of being in partnership with God to see His will come to pass in your life and in this earth.

PRAYER

Lord, teach me to pray the prayers of Your heart for myself and others in every situation. May the desires of my heart never be in conflict with the desires of Yours. Give me a love for Your Word and help me to use it to renew my mind. Thank You that in times of uncertainty I can depend on Your Holy Spirit to help me pray!

The Way to Freedom

Therefore, since Christ suffered in his body, arm yourselves also with the same attitude, because he who has suffered in his body is done with sin. As a result, he does not live the rest of his earthly life for evil human desires, but rather for the will of God.

1 PETER 4:1,2

In these verses, the apostle Peter urges us to follow Christ's example in choosing to suffer rather than fail to please God. Peter says that when we suffer in our bodies (or our "flesh"), sin loses its power over us. He's speaking of dying to our own will and submitting to God's. If I told you that you could be free from your sinful habits if you suffered for a while first, would you do it? Aren't you already suffering while you're at the mercy of your destructive behavior?

Let me share with you some things I've learned from undergoing this process of breaking free from a sinful habit or behavior. First, agree with God that you are sinning, because we have a tendency to lie to ourselves in order to continue our ungodly behavior. Then, repent with all your heart and ask for God's forgiveness every time you commit the sin. I find that this reinforces my shame over the offense and helps me to build up a holy determination which eventually enables me to break free. Call out to God and ask for His help. Sometimes I've done this many times a day, often with tears. Ask God what your part is in the process. Then take one or two steps to prove to God that you're serious about quitting. Keep your focus on Him. This is

one of the most impor-
tant steps to freedom.
Every time your focus
starts to shift to whatever
tempts you, immediately
bring it back to God, His
will and His Word. "The
weapons we fight with
are not the weapons of
the world. On the con-
trary, they have divine
power to demolish

LIVE ON PURPOSE TODAY

Put the following action
steps into practice when
dealing with sin:

1. Admit your sin.
2. Ask for forgiveness.
3. Memorize two Scriptures
   you can use to fight
   sin's temptation.

strongholds. We demolish arguments and every pretension that
sets itself up against the knowledge of God, and we take captive
every thought to make it obedient to Christ" (2 Cor. 10:4,5).
When we're tempted to sin, our minds will often try to come up
with reasons to justify our sinful behavior. If we don't reject these
thoughts immediately, we will act on them. We will never be able
to control our behavior if we don't control our thoughts. It takes
practice, but with God's help it can be done. "Remember that the
temptations that come into your life are not different from what
others experience. And God is faithful. He will keep the temptation from becoming so strong that you can't stand up against it.
When you are tempted, he will show you a way out so that you
will not give in to it" (1 Cor. 10:13 NLT). God has promised us a
way out of every temptation. Look for it. Sometimes your escape
will involve avoiding certain people, places, or things. Remember
that every time you resist temptation, sin's hold on you grows
weaker and it becomes easier for you to resist the next time. The
only way we can fail in this process is to quit and give up.
Instead, let's adopt the attitude of the apostle Paul when he said,
"By no means do I count myself an expert in all of this, but I've

got my eye on the goal, where God is beckoning us onward—to Jesus. I'm off and running, and I'm not turning back"! (Phil. 3:13,14 MESSAGE).

PRAYER

Lord, I ask that You bring to light the sins You want me to deal with at this time. Teach me how to die to my own will and to live according to Yours. Remind me that it's not always Satan tempting me, but it's often my own evil desires. (James 1:14.) Thank You that "I can do everything God asks me to with the help of Christ who gives me the strength and power"! (Phil. 4:13 TLB).

Pursue Perseverance

> *Pursue righteousness, godliness, faith,*
> *love, perseverance and gentleness.*
>
> 1 TIMOTHY 6:11 NASB

When my oldest son, Joseph, was in high school, he attended his first "See You at the Pole" event. That's when students and faculty are invited to gather around the school flagpole and pray for their school, their nation, and others. The event was scheduled for 7:00 A.M. that morning, but when Joseph awakened that day, he was so overcome with fear and anxiety that he became sick to his stomach. Knowing it was an attack from the enemy, he "set his face like flint" to do the will of God (Isa. 50:7). Joseph attended "See You at the Pole" that day, and he made many new Christian friends at that gathering who would enrich his life for years to come. A few months later God used my son to launch the first successful Bible club his school ever had. Through his experiences as club leader, Joseph learned some valuable lessons about perseverance. There were many times when he would work hard preparing for a meeting, only to have a handful of kids show up. We talked and prayed about it, and Joseph resolved that he would continue to hold weekly meetings, even if just one person showed up. God rewarded my son by blessing his efforts and using his club to touch and change the lives of hundreds of kids over the next several years. Joseph's testimony is proof that God's promise in Galatians 6:9 is true: "Let us not get tired of doing what is right, for after a while we will reap a harvest of blessing if we don't get discouraged and give up."

The dictionary defines *persevere* as "To continue in some effort, course of action, in spite of difficulty, opposition; be steadfast in purpose."[5] I like to think of it as a "holy determination," born of the Holy Spirit. The Bible talks a lot about perseverance, because without it we could never fulfill our God-given purpose. In Luke 8:15, in the parable of the seed sower, Jesus says, "But the seed on good soil stands for those with a noble and good heart, who hear the Word, retain it, and by persevering produce a crop." Perseverance will enable us to be fruitful for God. It will aid us in holding on to God's promises and obeying His Word when times get tough and we're tempted to lose heart. The author of Hebrews says it this way: "You need to persevere so that when you have done the will of God, you will receive what he has promised" (Heb. 10:36). Scripture says that if we want to be effective witnesses for Christ, we need to "watch our lives and doctrine closely" and "persevere in them" (1 Tim. 4:16). Let's face it—lukewarm Christianity isn't going to do much to change the world. Unbelievers don't want to just hear about Jesus, they want to see Jesus in us, and that calls for a holy determination. And what about prayer? Luke 18:1 says, "One day, Jesus told his disciples a story to illustrate their need for constant prayer, and to show them that they must never give up." When we are persistent in prayer, we can literally wear the devil out and stop

LIVE ON PURPOSE TODAY

Reverse the tendency to quit with a new attitude of determination. If you are discouraged about a particular task, take a moment to think about what the end will look like once you complete your job. Allow yourself to be encouraged that if you don't quit, you will win.

him in his tracks. The Bible teaches that perseverance is developed in us through "suffering" (Rom. 5:3) and "the testing of our faith" (James 1:3). Each time we resist temptation and walk in obedience instead of giving up or giving in, we strengthen our resolve to do God's will and to walk in the victory that Jesus bought for us on Calvary. In Revelation 2:3, Jesus commends His people's steadfastness: "You have persevered and have endured hardships for My name, and have not grown weary." Jesus never said it would be easy—He just said it would be worth it! When weariness threatens to overwhelm us in trying times, we can call on our God "who gives perseverance and encouragement" to give us the grace to endure, and eventually triumph (Rom. 15:5 NASB). James 5:11 talks about the blessings Job reaped as a result of his perseverance. Here's how The Message Bible puts it: "What a gift life is to those who stay the course! You've heard, of course, of Job's staying power, and you know how God brought it all together for him at the end. That's because God cares, cares right down to the last detail"!

PRAYER

Lord, give me the perseverance I need to do Your will so that I can receive the fulfillment of Your promises. Enable me to "run with perseverance the race marked out for me" (Heb. 12:1). When weariness threatens to overwhelm me, strengthen and refresh me, according to Your Word. (Ps. 68:9; Isa. 40:29.) Thank You that as I refuse to give up, I'll reap a harvest of blessings!

Fulfilling Our
God-Given Purpose

*For we are God's workmanship, created in Christ Jesus to do
good works, which God prepared in advance for us to do.*

EPHESIANS 2:10

Since my son John was a young teenager, he earnestly wanted
to make a difference for God. The Lord led him to start a
Christian Web site, Jesusfreakhideout.com, when he was
only 16 years old, and it has steadily grown and reached more and
more people each year. Even so, he has wrestled with feelings of
discouragement and frustration from time to time. When he
shares these feelings with me, I do my best to encourage him and
to help him persevere. On one of these occasions recently, he was
pouring out his heart to me and asking questions like—"How can
I make a real difference when the grand scheme of things is so
big? Is all of my seemingly endless work worth it? Does it have a
point? Aren't there plenty of other people doing the same thing—
and better? If they're getting more rewards than I am, does that
mean I'm not on the right track? Sometimes I feel like I'm going
against the wind—uphill!"

I not only sympathized with my son, but I empathized with
him, too. I've often wrestled with many of these same feelings and
questions, and I was painfully aware of what he was going
through. After all, what am I doing for God that millions of other
people aren't? Not only are countless people doing the same thing
that I am, but many of them are doing it better, and achieving

bigger and better results. Sometimes I feel like just one more little fish in a big sea of other little fish. On days when I let these things get me down, I try to remind myself of some uplifting truths that the Lord has taught me over the years. One of them is that I have been created by God with a very specific purpose in mind, and that He has prepared good works for me that only I can do. The Bible says, "For we are God's workmanship, created in Christ Jesus to do good works, which God prepared in advance for us to do" (Eph. 2:10). The Lord has prepared for me achievements that only I can accomplish in this life. Even the most gifted person in the world cannot accomplish my personal God-given assignments. It's entirely possible that there are lost people on this earth who will only be reached by me, as I carry out my God-given purpose and destiny. That fact alone is usually enough to keep me going when I'm tempted to quit and give up.

I've discovered that it's easy for me to lose my focus if I concentrate too much on what other people are doing. But if I stay focused on fulfilling the call of God on my own life, I can persevere in the toughest of times. I remind myself that God didn't create me to copy or imitate anyone else. He created me to fulfill my own unique God-given purpose and potential. And I can only do that by earnestly seeking His will for my life—by living each day in total dependence upon Him, and being sensitive and obedient to His Spirit's leading in all things. Scripture

LIVE ON PURPOSE TODAY

Articulate your God-given purpose in life to your spouse or close friend today. New vigor will rise up as you hear yourself share your own vision, and you'll be ready to run with it!

says, "The Lord will fulfill His purpose for me" (Ps. 138:8). As I concentrate on living for God and doing His will, I can count on Him to guide my steps in the paths that He has marked out for me. And I know that it's only in these paths that I will find the peace, joy, fulfillment, and success that are mine in Christ.

One thing's for sure—the devil does *not* want us to fulfill our God-given purpose and potential. He knows that if we do, we will wreak havoc on his kingdom of darkness, and we will be able to keep his interference in our lives to a minimum. He also knows that God will move heaven and earth to see that we receive all the good things He has in store for us. If it's your heart's desire to become all that God created you to be and to accomplish all the things He prepared for you in advance, please know that He will equip you with everything you need to succeed. I can't promise that you won't experience times of doubt or discouragement. But I *can* promise that if you'll keep your eyes on God and follow His lead, He will move mountains to make sure that His highest purposes for your life prevail!

PRAYER

Lord, today I offer You all that I am and all that I have.
I ask You to equip me with everything I need to fulfill my
God-given purpose and potential. Help me not to focus on
what others are doing, but to focus on You and Your call on
my life. Send me special encouragement when I get discouraged
or doubtful. Thank You that as I continually seek to follow
Your will for my life, I will enjoy divine favor, victory, and success!

Endnotes

1 *Webster's New World Thesaurus*, 3d. ed. (New York: Macmillan, 1997 Simon & Schuster), s.v. "anxiety."

2 *Merriam-Webster OnLine Dictionary*, copyright © 2002, s.v. "expect"; available from <http://www.m-w.com>.

3 *Webster's New World Thesaurus*, 3d. ed. (New York: Macmillan, 1997 Simon & Schuster), s.v. "expect."

4 *Merriam-Webster OnLine Dictionary*, copyright © 2002, s.v. "self-pity"; available from <http://www.m-w.com>.

5 *Webster's New World College Dictionary*, 3d. ed., (New York: Macmillan, 1997 Simon & Schuster), s.v. "persevere."

Prayer of Salvation

God loves you—no matter who you are, no matter what your past. God loves you so much that He gave His one and only begotten Son for you. The Bible tells us that "...whoever believes in him shall not perish but have eternal life" (John 3:16). Jesus laid down His life and rose again so that we could spend eternity with Him in heaven and experience His absolute best on earth. If you would like to receive Jesus into your life, say the following prayer out loud and mean it from your heart.

Heavenly Father, I come to You admitting that I am a sinner. Right now, I choose to turn away from sin, and I ask You to cleanse me of all unrighteousness. I believe that Your Son, Jesus, died on the cross to take away my sins. I also believe that He rose again from the dead so that I might be forgiven of my sins and made righteous through faith in Him. I call upon the name of Jesus Christ to be the Savior and Lord of my life. Jesus, I choose to follow You and ask that You fill me with the power of the Holy Spirit. I declare that right now I am a child of God. I am free from sin and full of the righteousness of God. I am saved in Jesus' name. Amen.

If you prayed this prayer to receive Jesus Christ as your Savior for the first time, please contact us on the Web at **www.harrisonhouse.com** to receive a free book.

Or you may write to us at
Harrison House
P.O. Box 35035
Tulsa, Oklahoma 74153

About the Author

J. M. Farro, gifted writer and author, reaches out to thousands of people through **www.jesus freakhideout.com**. Since 1996, this popular web site has grown in scope and outreach beyond the boundaries of the Christian music  industry. Their focus is album reviews, artist information, interviews, music news, and ministry through devotionals and prayer. On staff since 1998, J. M. Farro counsels thousands of men and women around the globe each year through her devotionals and prayer ministry. She and her husband, Joe, have two sons. They make their home in Nazareth, Pennsylvania.

To contact J.M. Farro, please write to:

J. M. Farro
P.O. Box 434
Nazareth, PA 18064

Or you may email her at:
farro@jesusfreakhideout.com
or jmf@jmfarro.com

Please include your prayer requests and comments when you write.

Other Books by J.M. Farro

Life on Purpose™ Devotional for Women
Life on Purpose™ Devotional

www.harrisonhouse.com

Fast. Easy. Convenient

- ◆ New Book Information
- ◆ Look Inside the Book
- ◆ Press Releases
- ◆ Bestsellers

- ◆ Free E-News
- ◆ Author Biographies
- ◆ Upcoming Books
- ◆ Share Your Testimony

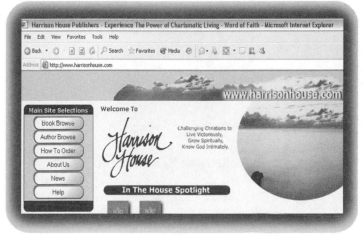

For the latest in book news and author information, please visit us on the Web at www.harrisonhouse.com. Get up-to-date zpictures and details on all our powerful and life-changing products. Sign up for our e-mail newsletter, *Friends of the House,* and receive free monthly information on our authors and products including testimonials, author announcements, and more!

Harrison House—
Books That Bring Hope, Books That Bring Change

The Harrison House Vision

Proclaiming the truth and the power

Of the Gospel of Jesus Christ

With excellence;

Challenging Christians to

Live victoriously,

Grow spiritually,

Know God intimately.